# It's All About The Bacon

## A PROVEN PROCESS FOR DRAWING MEN INTO LONG-TERM MINISTRY

Kevin Herrick

Copyright © 2023 Kevin Herrick

All rights reserved. No part of this book may be used or reproduced by any means, graphic, electronic, or mechanical, including photocopying, recording, taping, or by any information storage retrieval system without the written permission of the publisher except in the case of brief quotations embodied in critical articles and reviews.

Scriptures are taken from the New International Version English Standard Version, and the Amplified Version of the Bible

Books may be ordered through booksellers or by contacting:
Kevin Herrick
Kevin@mucmen.com
https://mucmen.com

Raising The Standard International Publishing

ISBN: 9781960641014

Printed in the United States of America
Edition Date: April 2023

# PREFACE
# MEN UNDER CONSTRUCTION

Would you say yes to an idea that could save your organization thousands of dollars while at the same time producing a high level of spiritual commitment in the men of your church?

I did. And boy, am I glad that I did!

Kevin was our facilities manager. He came to us from a career managing paint stores. One day he proposed an idea to me that he called "MUC," which stands for Men Under Construction. I could see the potential of a bunch of men bringing their skill sets to bear the physical needs of the church. At the time, we were retrofitting an old indoor tennis club to be used to do ministry as our church was growing. There were walls to build and offices to create. These men did that and much more. They made stages and props for our Christmas and Easter productions as well as what was needed for our weekly worship services. As you read this book, you'll discover that our MUC group has completed hundreds of thousands of dollars of work. That was a huge selling point for me, and I was pretty sure that Kevin could deliver the desired results.

What surprised me was the level of spiritual growth and loyalty I saw also developing. Kevin planned to lead a Bible study one week and then do construction projects the following week. The men worked side-by-side one week and sat in a big circle together with open Bibles the following week.

These men became friends and became vulnerable to each other. They developed as faithful disciples of Christ.

They went on mission trips together and helped others in the community.

By the time I retired as the church senior pastor, we hovered around 3000 in our worship services. The MUC group proved to be a very instrumental part of the overall church's health and success, and this same idea would also work in a church of 75... 200...or more.

Likewise, your church very likely has men who are underutilized physically and underdeveloped spiritually. They don't see themselves as Bible study leaders and don't want to be board members. They're mostly idle. The Men Under Construction concept could change that! I'm glad I said yes; chances are you will be too.

Read this book with an open heart and an eager mind. The men of your church will be glad you did!

*John Bray*
*Senior Pastor Heritage Church (Retired)*

# CONTENTS

| Chapter 1 | Introduction | 1 |
| --- | --- | --- |
| Chapter 2 | Statistics: The Importance Of Keeping Tract | 11 |
| Chapter 3 | Work Night Structure | 22 |
| Chapter 4 | Gathering The Materials | 28 |
| Chapter 5 | Setting The Guys Up For A Win | 30 |
| Chapter 6 | Partnering Up The Guys | 32 |
| Chapter 7 | Peace Before The Storm: Let The Work Begin | 35 |
| Chapter 8 | Work Nights: Knowing When To Call It | 38 |
| Chapter 9 | Providing Dessert And Fellowship | 40 |
| Chapter 10 | Having Good Spiritual Tools In Your Toolbox | 44 |
| Chapter 11 | Each Man Has Something To Offer | 46 |
| Chapter 12 | Our M.U.C. Policy: Keeping All Work At Heritage Properties | 51 |
| Chapter 13 | Props, Props, and More Props | 56 |
| Chapter 14 | Study Night Structure: Well, Sort Of | 74 |
| Chapter 15 | Finding The Right Study Topic For The Right Time | 78 |
| Chapter 16 | Developing A Spiritual Leadership Team (S.A.L.T. Team) | 85 |

| Chapter 17 | How To Celebrate And Acknowledge Each Other | 88 |
| --- | --- | --- |
| Chapter 18 | It's All About The Bacon | 93 |
| Chapter 19 | You're Always Welcome | 96 |
| Chapter 20 | What's Said At M.U.C. Stays At M.U.C | 103 |
| Chapter 21 | The Role Of The Leader | 108 |
| Chapter 22 | Know And Grow The Men In Your Group | 110 |
| Chapter 23 | The Short Version | 114 |
| | Notes | 125 |

## -1-
# Introduction

Think back to when you were a child when making friends was pretty easy. You would just go next door or down the street and hang out with your "new best friend," and you two would do all sorts of things together. Your circle of friends could also quickly expand based upon similar likings or their proximity to your house. You would grow to trust these friends, share stories and adventures, and their families became extensions of your own. As you grew into your teenage years, you never gave a thought to the ideas of what their social class was or how much money they made. You were more concerned about if they were mad at you for talking to a certain girl or what they were doing the following Friday night after the football game. Your social life was simple, and your circle of friends was not so complicated.

Eventually, you grew into a man, and your priorities naturally changed to focusing more on your career, spouse and family, possessions, and financial security. Your personal goals changed drastically from when you were a child, and the innocent free-spirited friendships of the past would seldom come your way again. But what if you could find that youthful kind of friendship again? What if you could freely share your stories without fear of judgment or retribution? What if you could find a group of friends like you had as a child? Remember the guys who had your back, not just occasionally, but consistently without reservation? Remember the men you could bounce ideas off while working side-by-side on purpose as you create opportunities for others to experience God's Kingdom through your friendships and perseverance?

Let's face it. As we got older and burdened with the responsibilities of life, we didn't trust like we used to, love like we used to, open up like we used to, and make friends as we should. That is exactly why I had to write this book.

This book is about developing Godly relationships through a proven process called "Men Under Construction" or the acronym M.U.C. We meet every Monday night year-round. We alternate one week as a work night and the next as a study night. Our goal is to serve God, the church, and each other using our skills, actions, and commitment to one another.

In our Men Under Construction group, we have learned to trust each other enough that we have willingly become vulnerable to each other. This trust didn't happen overnight, though. We toiled together, prayed together, told jokes, and made sarcastic comments about each other, and learned that through the supernatural love that The Holy Spirit provides, we could be whole again. The same way we were when we were still young children. As you digest this book, you will see how we have opened up to each other and allowed ourselves to have deep, trusting relationships again.

So What? Take the time to read this book. Think of the men in your church congregation who could benefit from your own Men Under Construction group. Make a wholehearted commitment to giving these ideas and concepts your best effort, and you, too, will see that there is hope for your generation and those men in the future who are just beginning to wonder what happened to their youth.

## On The Lighter Side:

We often joke that in order to be part of the Men Under Construction group, you need to have a dog, a beard, or a love of bacon. Sarcasm is the love language at MUC. If you don't speak it (or have a dog, a beard, or love bacon), then you don't get in. Honestly, though, it really comes down to only a few things. You simply need to be willing to work on your relationship with God and others and enjoy the sweet, savory taste of bacon.

## Notes About This Book And Author:

I am a simple guy, and like many other men, God gave me the gift of connecting easily with other men. I feel that I can talk and relate well to the average man because that's who I am. As you read through this book, you'll come across some of the little thought-provoking sayings I picked up from other guys, such as "So What?" or "So What Now?" and nicknames like "Muckleheads."

One of my long-time mentors and friends, Pastor John Bray, would always finish his sermon with a "So what now?" moment. It was John's way of focusing on that one thing that he wanted everyone to take home with them and ponder on mentally. That saying has always stuck with me because it's a perfect question to end a chapter or at the end of a study night. So, what now? What will you do with what you've learned or what we've all talked about?

Throwing questions such as that out to the guys helps not only to know that we all got something out of the study night subject but also to what intensity we got it! As for the term "Muckleheads," it is totally a term of endearment.

A beloved and lost member of MUC nicknamed us Muckleheads. We often humble ourselves by acknowledging that we're just a bunch of Muckleheads doing the best we can to figure life out. There's something about using the term that just screams, "Hey man, we're just a bunch of meek men who love our God and have a huge desire to serve together.

## Why "Men Under Construction" and its Name?

In November of 2003, when I started at our Heritage Wesleyan Church, the church was going through an explosive period of growth. It needed someone with strong management and maintenance experience to manage the property, work with contractors and do any and all maintenance. Heritage hired me to essentially be the general contractor on all projects needed to turn a retrofitted indoor tennis club into a fully functioning church building. We had an entire staff of janitorial and event set-up people but no real maintenance people besides me. It didn't take very long to realize that in order to maintain an aging facility, a group of volunteers would be needed to keep things moving along. So, after a year of struggling, I realized I needed help.

"Let's start a volunteer work group!" was my solution. However, I didn't want to have your typical men's work group.

Having been raised in the church environment, I had seen how difficult it was to create and maintain an effective men's group. I really felt within this group, there needed to be an element of relational connection and spiritual growth (not just for the other guys but also for me). I came up with the idea of having a men's group that not only worked around the church together but also did life together. I wanted to see true discipleship, complemented with some sort of men's type of Bible study. It then became obvious that creating an alternating weekly schedule of a "work night" one Monday night and "study night" the following Monday night just might fly.

While trying to come up with a name for this new group, I asked several of the assistants at the church for their opinion. One in particular, (Renee), came up with the name "Men Under Construction," followed by a good laugh at the acronym it represented, M.U.C. or "mucked up." I pondered on the title for about two minutes and immediately felt that this was a "keeper," so we had the name M.U.C. to build upon. The name felt so "God-inspired," and it was full of meaning. It really was that simple.

The next step was to put a notice in the weekly bulletin that the church was starting a "Men's group." We would hold our first gathering on Monday, October 15th, 2004, at 6:30 p.m. That Monday night, which was our very first study night, twelve guys showed up, and the rest was history.

## A Little More About Me:

I grew up in a typical family of five in the Midwest city of Rock Island, Illinois. I attended Catholic schools all the way up to my college years. When I was in eighth grade, my parents wanted a more evangelical experience, so we started attending an Assembly of God church. At first, I was pretty heavily immersed in this new church life. That was until I hit the age of nineteen, at which point I started to question everyone's motives for attending church, including my own. So, I stopped going to church. It wasn't that I ran from the church. It was more like I needed to discover who I was and could be without the church's influence. Throughout this "unchurched" period, I still felt God and I had a pretty good relationship.

I held an eclectic number of jobs. I was a mascot for a large pizza establishment and worked for a local True Value Hardware store for several years. I did a three-year apprenticeship with the Painters Union, built a house, and worked for a small general contractor. I also worked for one of the largest paint manufacturing companies in the world. During all this time, I still had a passion for connecting with other men. I enjoyed listening to their issues and occasionally gave guidance when asked.

At the age of twenty-seven (now married with two children), my wife and I started attending a small Wesleyan church in Moline, Illinois. The church seemed to be bulging at the seams, and the level of enthusiasm about future expectations of God was easy to see. Our Heritage church was looking into buying a 65,000-square-foot building, which was formerly a tennis and racquetball club. Under the guidance of Pastor John Bray and his wife Patty, the church would grow from 120 people to well over 3,000. The new building proved to be a huge blessing to our church family. This building would be an ideal home for the church to grow and prosper.

The church started a seasonal outreach program called "Creative Christmas." This production included traditional and contemporary Christmas songs, as well as interesting bends on some of the tunes we had all grown up with. Each show had a unique theme which was carried throughout the program, as well as skits that followed along with that theme. Being fairly crafty, I joined in to create the props needed for each year's production. In the early days of Creative Christmas, the show would be held at small venues, typically seating 300-400 people, so the props were pretty low-keyed. If only I had known what the future would hold! (See the section titled: "Props, Props, and More Props"). The Creative Christmas production grew to the point where we eventually sold out one of our best local venues for multiple nights, serving over 12,000 people.

Our Men Under Construction (MUC) group became the sole designer and builder of the event props. I feel that we helped the church to bring the Creative Christmas show to a level that expressed professionalism, high quality, and of course, extreme "Creativity."

**"Whatever you do, work at it with all your heart, as working for the Lord"**
**~Colossians 3:23 NIV~**

Back to October 2003. I held the position of branch manager of a paint store. At that time, the store was only a few years old, and we had a good reputation within the painting community. Unfortunately, my then-district manager attempted to force me to either burn myself out or quit.

At that same time, a full-time position had opened up at my church for someone with my life skills. My wife and I were volunteering to paint a considerable addition the church was working on when I interviewed for the facilities job. (We were painting the former tennis court area). I could tell immediately through the interview process that God was opening up this opportunity for me to step into.

Back at the paint store, I filed a complaint with the Human Resources department that my district manager was unjustly harassing me. A week later, the director of Human Resources and my district manager showed up to discuss the complaint that I had made. They were unaware that I had already decided to leave and had a letter of resignation ready.

    About an hour before that meeting, one of my friends from church "randomly" called me to tell me that he needed to pray for me, but he wasn't sure why. He prayed that whatever would happen that day, I would handle it with grace and allow it to be a witness to my faith. God knows I wanted to berate my district manager and tear him to shreds. However, thanks to the prayers, I maintained my composure and handled that day well. This event was truly a new beginning for me in fully listening and trusting the Holy Spirit to control my thoughts and actions. As for the guy who prayed for me, he later became one of the anchors of our church MUC group. Needless to say, I left the paint store job that day after I had said goodbye to my employees and contractors. I ripped off my tie that I was required to wear for the last 13 years, went home, and put on a pair of flip-flops, and I never looked back (I still wear flip-flops every day).

## That First Night

    So here we are, our first Men Under Construction night. Twelve guys were sitting around a couple of tables in a small room, which was once a slightly modified racquetball court, in an old building built in 1977. To start our first meeting, I chose to do an icebreaker with these new, mostly unknown men. The plan was to play a game called "Two Truths and a Lie" (appropriate for a church group). The first contestant wrote down, "I won the lottery, and I am now a millionaire," "I spent the last 15 years in prison," and "I got married for the first time at the age of 47." After reading this, I'm thinking to myself, "What kind of mess did

I get myself into?" At the time, I wasn't prepared to deal with any radical social issues, let alone someone fresh out of prison. Fortunately, the truth came out that this new friend had been an employee at our local prison and not a millionaire.

This new eclectic group we initially gathered consisted of one guy who was 82 years old, a guy who worked in Human Resources at a hospital, a highway paving company owner, a retired and non-retired truck driver, our prison worker, a teacher, a hospital maintenance worker, an Information Technology worker, a salesman, an insurance broker, a John Deere shop worker, and me.

That first night we shared ideas and dreams of what this group could do for our church (no one had any thoughts or visions of what the group would eventually do for each other). Most of the men were there primarily for the work portion, and they might only "tolerate" the proposed study portion. We could never have believed how much God would bless our friendships and create such a strong bond. It is a brotherhood that has flourished throughout all these years. Looking back, it was amazing how well we all worked together, especially with so many varied backgrounds, trials, and experiences.

For the record, out of the first twelve men we started MUC with, two have died, one didn't feel he fit well and left, but the rest of the guys are still actively participating to this day.

Of course, the spouses have also consistently been a big part of the group. They have played several roles in our success through their prayers, encouragement, and support of food and desserts. As you go through this guide, you'll occasionally see where the wife of one of the guys interjects their viewpoint for the group and reflects upon the positive impact that MUC has had on their husband and their marriage.

**Here Is A Note From One Of The MUC Spouses.**

My husband Bill is not a "joiner" by nature. It took some serious prodding to get him to attend that very first Monday meeting of Men Under Construction. Yes, it took a while, but he soon realized that it was where he belonged. MUC is a group that utilizes my husband's gifts and talents, unlike any other men's group that I've ever heard of. Bill is a handyman, willing to try anything but really talented in using power tools. His favorite night would be when he gets to use those tools to get things done. The amount of serious work that the MUC group has done, both big remodels and simple maintenance, is of enormous value to the church. Over the years, I have seen positive growth and change in Bill, and this group certainly is the most significant contributor to this change. The sheer diversity of the group is wonderful, and Bill has seen what Godly men are like in each and every meeting. It's true that it took nudging to get him to try MUC, but now he hates to miss a Monday night. Birthdays and anniversaries better not land on a Monday night! Signed: The wife of one of the original members of MUC.

**"Let us not neglect our Meeting Together, as some people do, but encourage one another, especially now that the day of His return is drawing near"**
**~ Hebrews 10:25 NIV~**

So now, let's move on to the logistics of M.U.C.

## -2-
# Statistics:
# The Importance Of Keeping Track

One of the major benefits of keeping track of our statistics and special events is that at some point, I would be asked by management, the Board of Administration, new pastors, or parishioners about the MUC group and what kind of impact it has had on the church. It's pretty easy to sell the group's vision once the stats are on the table. It also helps everyone understand that we are in this for the long haul and are a highly committed group of volunteers.

I have always liked to recognize special events such as birthdays and anniversaries. The first anniversary of our MUC fellowship was pretty memorable. By October 2005, we had already completed so many projects (and no one got seriously hurt either!) The group had grown from twelve to twenty-four men. We were developing strong friendships with one another and started relying upon each other for fellowship and accountability. We were becoming a real asset to the church, and I wanted the guys to tangibly see the results of their labor. We had poured many Monday nights into projects like building props and tearing apart portions of the building. Seeing all the areas we had been using our God-given skills was getting pretty easy. To create some sort of baseline to show the value of this volunteer work, I used a rudimentary system of assigning $25 per hour for each hour a man had committed during the work nights. The monetary benefits alone were proving invaluable.

On the "study nights," we went through two really intentional Bible studies, and the interactive atmosphere proved invaluable to our fellowship growth. People were starting to notice, and we had new guys starting to pop in every week. I had created an email address list so I could shoot out a note or reminder every Thursday about what was coming up on the following Monday night. I made a cake and a one-page flier that first anniversary night to pass out to the guys. This flier included the number of dollars saved in their volunteer labor; a listing of the guys who now called MUC their own; a mission statement; a listing of past and future projects; and pictures of the guys working hand in hand.

As of today, it's been nearly twenty years since we have been meeting together. We have spent over 400 study nights together and have gone through at least 60 study books. I've calculated that we have saved the church almost one-million dollars in labor expenses with over 34.000 volunteer man-hours since that first work night in 2004. Of course, I have adjusted for the cost of labor and goods since that first night. I now use $30 per hour as a base for the volunteer labor rate. In all these years together, we have eaten at least 700 pounds of steak and 2,000 pounds of bacon. Our average attendance (including our time through the COVID pandemic) has been 40 men for study nights and 26 men for work nights. There are now over 100 men who consider themselves a part of our Men Under Construction group (active or inactive).

During a long stretch of growth at Heritage church, Bob Crawford was our Executive Pastor. Bob came to us with the knowledge and experience that would typically be unobtainable in a church arena. I learned so much from Bob about validating our efforts and being as intentional as possible. But the best schooling I learned was to make each word count. This is such an invaluable lesson. Below is a note from Bob about the guys and how he saw the effects of our MUC group.

## Letter from Bob Crawford

Men Under Construction. There are two areas that most churches could benefit from a group such as M.U.C. First: increased volunteer participation, especially in the skilled labor arena, and second, higher engagement with adult men. The Men Under Construction (M.U.C.) ministry does both for our Heritage Church. Over the years, the expenses saved and avoided by having this group have reached hundreds of thousands of dollars. They allowed us to have professional-level sets for worship that we would never otherwise be able to afford.

Further, during major construction, building refurbishments, or landscaping projects, we avoided considerable contractor expenses by self-performing the duties with our limited staff and outstanding team of volunteers.

While the business piece has been so valuable to the church, it is not the most critical piece of the ministry. The deep spiritual connections these men have formed as a "small group" is priceless. Their commitment and loyalty to each other are so strong. It is fair to say that each man's personal faith in God has deepened during their involvement in M.U.C.

Leaders have grown to become better leaders. Nothing shows this growth more than talking to the wives of the men involved to see how their husbands (and thus their entire families) have been positively impacted. Another

example is when a tragedy (significant life event) happens; to see how this group of men responds and supports is priceless!
*Bob Crawford*
*Executive Pastor Heritage Church (Retired)*

## So What?

We intentionally don't seek recognition from the congregation or actually from anyone. This attitude being the case, the only affirmation the guys get is from each other. Honestly, this is the best scenario, as too much recognition can create the wrong kind of pride. As men with hearts bent toward serving, we need to be humble and understand that even though it may be unrecognized by man, God sees what we are doing, and He has continued to bless our efforts.

> **"Whoever serves me must follow me; and where I am, my servant also will be. My Father will honor the one who serves me."**
> **~John 12:26 NIV~**

## Be Prepared for Both the Good and Bad

Always be prepared and amazed for both the good moments as well as the not-so-good moments as your group grows and strong bonds between the men begin to form. It seems like every time we get together, there are always brief flashes of both the good and the bad.

The bad moments are when you learn that one of your guys just found out their spouse filed for a divorce, or they recently visited the doctor and received a bad prognosis. When one of these "bad events" occur, it can create an opportunity to see how powerful our God is and how supportive our group can be for one another. While on the other hand, when a "good news" event pops up, such as a positive doctor report or an estranged family member has been reconciled, it's easy to recognize it as an opportunity to celebrate and to give praise to God for His grace, mercy, and miracles. I must admit that there seem to be more good moments than bad, and I thank God for that! However, any of these good or bad moments should always be seen as an opening to get the group to connect with each other. Often, these moments provide opportunities for prayer and a deeper connection to one another.

***"In all things God works for the good of those who love him, who have been called according to his purpose."***
***~ Romans 8:28~***

Over the years, two stories stand out and have become part of our MUC story about how God worked in both good and bad situations. The first story is about how I screwed up, but God used my "oops" for His good. The second story is one of my greatest losses, but the Holy Spirit showed His presence through it all.

## God's Timing

Have you ever made a stupid mistake and yet had the Holy Spirit use that mistake for good?

About nine months after we started the MUC group, we were having an incredible study night. It was a beautiful Spring evening, so we met outside on the front patio of the church. There was a sizable table and chairs that we all gathered around for the meeting. We were a few weeks into an accountability study that pushed some of the men's mental, emotional, relational, and spiritual boundaries and opened up some great dialogue.

We finished the study around 9:30 p.m. and headed directly to our vehicles. It was such a special night. On the way to our vehicles, I got sidetracked by one of the guys who needed a more in-depth conversation about conviction he felt because of the subject matter in the study. I got so wrapped up in the conversation that I inadvertently left my Bible, along with some additional study books and a bank bag with some cash in it. I left it all lying on the table on the patio. Bright and early the following day after arriving at work, I was hunted down by our Children's Pastor named Jim. Jim had my Bible, the books, and the money bag in his hand. I immediately realized what I had done and exclaimed that I totally forgot to grab those when we finished last night. Jim proceeded to tell me that the book within that stack of items had saved a guy's life last night! Now Jim really had my attention as I tried to think, "What could have possibly happened?" So, here's where God used my forgetfulness to help save a man's soul.

After we left, a guy showed up with the intent to commit suicide on the front patio of the church in order to make a huge negative statement against the church. You see, the brother of this suicidal man had come on staff at the church two years prior. This distraught man had gathered up his family a year earlier and followed his brother from their hometown in West Virginia to Rock Island, Illinois, to be closer to his brother. This young man had a job working as an Emergency Medical Service technician. He had two little girls and a wife.

Earlier in the day, when he got home from work to his wife and family, his wife told him that their marriage was over, and she was taking the two girls and leaving him.

The fellow was so distraught and confused. He rationalized that the whole reason for his mess was because of his brother and the church. So, he decided he couldn't take it any longer and would end his life in a public church location to show his brother and the congregation how they had failed him. So, he showed up at the church, distraught, hurt, and wanting the pain to end. He walked up onto the patio and sat at the same table we had been sitting at earlier. However, instead of committing suicide, he picked up the book we had been studying and started reading. He read that study book from cover to cover.

For "some reason," Pastor Jim decided to come in early that Tuesday morning. Upon arriving at church, Pastor Jim found this poor, anguished young man sitting on the front patio with tears streaming down his face. We all had been praying for this guy for quite some time that somehow, he would come to know the peace and assurance that a relationship with the Lord can truly gain. That morning this hurting soul turned over his pain to Jesus Christ.

What did I learn? God is always in control, and there really isn't any such thing as a coincidence. I learned never to give up on the amazing power of prayer and that this would be just the first miracle of countless moments where God would show up in ways I never imagined.

**Danny's Story-**
**Still dealing with the loss.**

Danny started coming to Men Under Construction on day one. He was a local railroad train engineer and always had some interesting stories about the railroad and some of the odd things he'd seen as he traveled from railroad yard to railroad yard. Danny was one of the most genuine guys I've ever met. If he were down and out, you'd know it. If he were having a good day, you'd know it too. Danny was also one of the most generous guys to cross our paths. He would always open his house up to anyone.

He also had a beautiful in-ground swimming pool that he loved to share with his grandkids and anyone who wanted to take a dip.

The MUC guys took a few mission trips to Haiti with the intent of working on Wesleyan churches that needed help after the January 2010 earthquakes. Danny decided to join us on one of these trips to Jacmel, Haiti. Our task was to build a church in the quake-ravaged village of Sus La Matra, Haiti.

On this particular mission trip, we needed to make a trek of about a mile uphill from the road, which was as far as the truck could take us. We were immediately met by the children of this hillside village of around 120 people. Of course, they were excited to see the "Bwa" (white), as they would call us. Danny, in particular, was one of the guys the kids latched on to immediately since he had flowing white hair and a solid white beard (just imagine a skinny Santa Claus). Danny never got much construction work done on these trips, mainly because the locals were captivated by his warm smile and friendly demeanor. He spent most of the time building relationships and doing his best to bridge the obvious language barrier of our team. Often, I'd look up and see him playing with the kids, just like Danny was one of them. He would run and chase balls, never letting his age or physical abilities hinder the moment.

Danny could relate so well to anyone. He was one of those guys who naturally attracted people into his world because of his honesty and his openness.

## It's All About The Bacon

Danny was often our guinea pig when testing props for big church event productions. One year we built a monorail type of track along the ceiling of the sanctuary that would transfer a person from the back of the venue to the main stage about 12 feet off the ground. Danny being the great volunteer that he always was, strapped on the safety harness for the trolley and, without any regard for bodily injury, Danny flew like an angel playing the "air guitar" the whole way. He totally trusted those of us who designed and built that flying rig.

During another Christmas production, we built this rather sizable wood platform set on large, concealed pneumatic tires. This platform was supposed to travel from the back of the main aisle all the way up to the stage of the venue where we were holding the performance. Since it was too complicated to make this platform motorized and remote-controlled, we recruited Danny to be our motor. Danny was responsible for maneuvering the stage piece with a singer standing on it. The singer would then appear to be floating smoothly down the aisle via this platform.

Danny was to climb inside the platform and use two little peepholes and a laser light as a guide. Then gently move the stage piece from here to there while on his knees using his head and a shoulder harness attached under the prop. The first run and the following few practices went so smoothly. Danny was right on his mark, and his timing was impeccable. The afternoon prior to the actual event, though, we got Danny good. During the final rehearsal, the singer climbed on the box, Danny pushed off, then further down the aisle, one by one, a MUC guy mounted onto the stage piece until six of us and the singer were on board. Danny did make it to the main stage, and all I can say is that I never knew he could sweat that much! He was such a good trooper once he found out how we pranked him.

Danny was always optimistic about getting things done and how God gave us the skills we needed to succeed. About 7-8 years into being a "Mucklehead" (which was the nickname he referred to all of us as), Danny got a divorce from his wife of many years. During that time, he believed there was no way to salvage his marriage, and he started slipping into an overwhelming depression. It was obvious to the guys what was happening, so we all took the time to reach out to him.

We'd drop into his house to take him out for dinner. We even took weekend trips together to see a familiar friend (a MUC guy who moved to Missouri). Danny always said, "I'm tired and don't know how much longer I can go on."

Danny had a dog named Izzy, who was his closest companion throughout this devastating time. She was such a unique dog, but as all pets do, she died, leaving Danny even more distraught. Danny finally ended his pain in the fall of 2018. I can remember that day very vividly. I was at work when the Senior Pastor found me and told me what had happened. I really felt lost for quite a while afterward, and I still get teary-eyed just thinking about him. There are very few people that you'll ever come across like Danny. He really loved God and us too, but he just couldn't accept the hand that life had dealt him.

## So What?

Never take anyone for granted, and never give up on each other. I never thought Danny would end his own life. Even though he frequently seemed down and out, he always had a smile on his face and still did his best to make you feel welcome. There were multiple times we would pray for mental healing so that Danny could find some peace. However, looking back, I realize that Danny never seemed to accept the gift of forgiveness. I'll never really know the whole story. However, I look forward to meeting him again in Heaven. I miss you, Danny, but I wouldn't trade knowing you for anything else.

*"For to me, to live is Christ and to die is gain."*
*~Philippians 1:21 NIV~*

## -3-
# Work Night Structure

When the MUC idea first hit me, I realized we needed help maintaining our church properly. I felt like the best solution would be to gather the men together to volunteer one night to do projects and then see what adding a Bible study might look like (but it wasn't the preference of many of the men initially). We then chose to alternate work nights with study nights. I will do my best to explain the basics of each individual night and how they are structured.

We will start with the work night, which begins with prayer, and deciding how we implement the projects for the MUC ministry.

**Identifying All the Projects**

It's nice to have two weeks between work nights. This time allows me to move throughout our properties and look for what needs repair. I'm confident that you would also discover this timing to be an advantage once you've got some of the structure in place. At our church, we have implemented a computer-based work ticket program. Using this work ticket program makes it easy to identify projects because everyone on staff is now a pair of discerning eyes. Anyone, including parishioners, can put in a ticket for anything that is damaged or broken. The majority of items that come up through the work ticket system would be tasks such as changing light bulbs, replacing damaged ceiling tiles, extracting dirt from carpets, fixing toilets, and a lot of general maintenance issues. If your church has a small staff or lacks folks with discerning eyes, I suggest you take your guys through the property and identify potential projects at least once a quarter as a group.

We also have a lot of seasonal projects that we focus on at various times of the year. Tasks include putting down and spreading mulch, cleaning, and organizing the garage, trimming trees and bushes, cleaning and repairing fleet vehicles, changing furnace filters, and cleaning general grounds.

In addition, we will always have medium to large construction projects to work on, which tends to happen with a growing congregation and multiple properties.

Tasks such as: removing walls (everyone loves demolition!), building walls and stages, installing doors, or creating new openings in walls, building stairs, and the list goes on and on. Of course, a majority of these larger construction projects would have been planned out well in advance so a scope of work, budget, and timeline could be established.

During the Christmas, Easter, and Fall seasons, we would have a whole different set of projects primarily designed around props and stage design. Regarding props, the Worship Arts people would come to me with a list of things they'd want to see.

Their job is to dream big, and our job is to make it happen. Some of these props were fairly complex, so we (the MUC guys) would have a brainstorming meeting where everyone who attended that night would have a chance to weigh in on an idea. We often devised a basic concept to get any project started. Seeing how these small ideas can grow into a fully functioning prop or stage project design is always exciting. Other times a few of our projects would require a "project meeting" in advance of the work. Or we would sometimes discuss ideas for the upcoming work night during a "housekeeping" moment before starting a study night if needed.

On the evening of a work night, I'd typically have a rough drawing or whiteboard sketch of what the stage or prop is supposed to look like, then the magic would happen. Even in the midst of the construction, everyone would still have a chance to weigh in on how we could improve on the plan or make the idea better. A few of our guys had engineering backgrounds, so using their skills and experience would frequently take the prop to the "next level" of design. (In other words, try to recruit an engineering type of guy from your congregation). I've learned that retired engineers love to jump in when asked. But also realize that not every work night has to be some sort of astronomical event. We've had nights where we just worked on cutting, sanding, and staining simple wood crosses slated to be passed out during the next baptism.

During one of our Creative Christmas productions, we were asked to recreate the lower portion of the touring stage from the Irish rock group U2. (from the U2360 tour) However, our stage version would need to be built on top of an existing 40' by 60' stage structure already set up at the venue. Also, to make the requirements for this show even more interesting, we were asked to design three full-scale versions of the Blue Man Group Thongophone and figure out how to make two guys appear to fall through the roof of the venue to the stage. Then the men were to jump up and sing while holding a "snowzooka" (a prop similar to a bazooka but air-driven and shot plastic balls over a hundred feet into the audience). Because of these exciting challenges, we had a MAJOR brainstorming exercise.

## It's All About The Bacon

For the U2-style stage, we decided the best route was to build a series of trestles (like a train track trestle) that we could space out to accommodate the various heights of the existing floor and stage. We pre-built our stage portion in the church's parking lot to ensure we had all our measurements close. We then loaded everything into a semi-trailer and hauled it to the venue location. On Monday night, we assembled the stage, starting at 5:00 p.m. and finishing at 4:00 a.m. We were under an extremely tight timeline since we had one day to set up, followed by days of practice and three full days of performances.

The Thongophone was a blast to design and build. We started by constructing three five-foot frames out of wood that would each hold a series of three-inch plastic tubing vertically. The bottom of these tubes was all bent and formed to produce a specific octave of sound. To create an actual sound, a flip flop (or foot thong) was glued to the end of a drumstick and then slapped onto the top hole of the tubing. By the time we placed all three Thongophones together, we had a full keyboard (61 keys or tubes in total).

As for the guys who fell from the ceiling, all I can say is that it involved a few stagehands dropping blow-up dolls dressed like our two hosts 60' from the roof to a heavy rolling fog that was slowly rolled down on top of the stage. Once the "dummies" landed in the fog, the real dummies who lay in wait under the fog jumped up, dusted themselves off, and promptly began to sing a song called "Snowball Fight." It was amazing to see.

## So What?

Every man's time is essential. So, establishing the project workload for each work night is imperative, and most work nights have been very successful as a result. However, there have been a handful of times when we have canceled the work night because there wasn't enough work to keep everyone busy for a few hours. Although that's not the preferred thing to do, it happens. However, if you think creatively, you'd be surprised by what you can come up with.

**"Plans fail for lack of counsel, but with many advisers they succeed."**
**~Proverbs 15:22~**

## -4-
# Gathering The Materials

I find gathering the materials the most time-consuming effort for setting up a work night. Even if I had created a thorough list of items I needed from the hardware store, finding everything to make the work night successful has always been challenging. So don't become frustrated if you find yourself in a similar predicament. Thankfully, we are blessed to have several big box hardware stores in our local community. One, in particular, is known as Menards. My saying about Menards is, "If Menards doesn't have it, then you probably didn't need it." This hardware store has enough stuff that a reasonably creative person can make anything happen. My biggest issue is imagining something and then assuming it's actually made. I've found this problem happens especially around the Christmas season when the parts for the props and stage pieces we are asked to build just don't exist.

Nonetheless, we always figure something out. If you're in a smaller town with only your hometown hardware store, don't give up, there's always a pathway around whatever kind of mountain you'll come up to. I worked for True Value Hardware for seven years. The folks that work at those smaller stores are typically pretty ingenious. Don't be shy about asking questions and relying upon their skills and experience. Just remember that creativity is a must! So never give up. Even when we try and build something, and it fails, we still find that the process eventually takes us to a completed, successful project.

Here are a few trinkets of thoughts and ideas that have served us well in MUC. We created a closet space within each property that houses tools, fasteners, light bulbs, filters, ballasts, paint, tape, and other general supplies we often need. All the guys know that this supply room can make the difference between project completion with or without frustration. We also designated a place in our garages for extra lumber storage. Lumber and scraps can take over any storage space; we have limited our saved lumber size to be no shorter than 4 feet in length.

On a few occasions, we turned to Facebook Marketplace to see if anyone in the area was selling what we needed. We have found siding, shingles, plywood, doors, and even the parts and pieces for several of the props we had to make. Keeping our eyes open for alternative means has helped us create substantial savings and effort.

## So What?

On the day of every work night meeting, I'll spend several hours gathering the materials we need. Although it can be frustrating to invest hours into finding that "perfect" piece, or enough of those hard-to-locate parts, it will truly make or break the overall success of each minute the group invests. The following section is about setting the men up for success. Gathering the right stuff needed is a great start.

*"Commit your work to the Lord, and your plans will be established."*
*~Proverbs 16:3 ESV~*

## -5-
## Setting The Guys Up For A Win!

Personally, I think I have an attention deficit issue. I sometimes even believe squirrels are running all over the building, trying to steal my attention. So, to ensure we are prepared for the work night, I will write out these thoughts and record them on my phone when I think of an item, tool, or process. Anything I can do to get things staged and laid out for the projects at hand, far enough ahead of time without forgetting where I was heading, will assist in the success of the work meeting. I'll gather extension cords, tools, ladders, building materials, etc. It doesn't matter if it's applying mulch to the landscaping, changing out light bulbs, or building 6' tall ornaments for the Christmas season. I have learned that if you want to be successful and utilize every minute of each guy's time, you must do your best to prepare for the job ahead of time.

Since our MUC meeting times are on Mondays, I would spend significant time making detailed notes for supplies. This time includes traveling to our local hardware stores to procure the supplies we need, stage an area for each task, and sometimes I make sketches of the prop or stage piece and add it to the pile of supplies. Since not every man knows the property's layout, I might also add a copy of the interior design of the building along with the required staged supplies. A star or an arrow on that paper map allows for more independence and less chance for the wrong item to be repaired. Ultimately the idea is to ensure that whoever shows up to the work night is given enough supplies and tools to get started. I don't always succeed like

I would like to, but often this would still lend towards more creativity and out-of-the-box thinking, leading eventually to a well-done project. Being flexible is key. I frequently repeat," **The right guys showed up for the right project at the right time!"** After doing this for the past 20 years, my trust in God's provision has never EVER been let down.

## So What?

There can never be enough planning and preparation. If you find yourself overwhelmed by these tasks, then lean on another one of the guys for assistance. There is nothing wrong with splitting a project into parts and having help with each element.

*"And my God will supply every need of yours according to his riches in glory in Christ Jesus."*
*~Philippians 4:19 ESV~*

## -6-
# Partnering Up The Guys Together

In the last section, I briefly mentioned that it's ok to split projects up and have a different leader for each task. We have been practicing this strategy since day one. The idea is to know your men well enough that natural leaders will emerge through the challenges. Get to know what sort of talents and skills each man can bring to the field. In our group, every project (doesn't matter how small) will have at least two men on it. Obviously, the camaraderie is invaluable, but by teaming guys up together, a sort of "Journeyman and Apprentice" scenario gets formed.

Once everyone is gathered at our property and the men are ready to begin, I would review the list of projects and then start teaming the guys together. Although this doesn't always work perfectly, most of the time, it feels like God's hand is on the night. The only time this process really got screwed up was during a Christmas prop build night. I had put together three guys (one who knew carpentry well, and the other two were fantastic laborers). My mistake was that all three of these men were left-handed, and I wasn't aware of that. At the time, we were building eight-foot-tall trees made of 2x2 lumber. The process was to create something similar to a teepee. Then starting at the bottom of the teepee, a six-foot board would be laid horizontally. Next, another horizontal board would be placed on top of the previous 2x2, except this board would be an inch shorter, and a spiral pattern would start to emerge (like a spiral staircase).

It's All About The Bacon

This pattern would continue until all that was left was a four-inch spot at the top of the tree where all of the vertical 2x2s would gather. The issue was that all right-handed men made their trees counterclockwise, but the left-handed men made their trees clockwise! No one really noticed it, but we occasionally joke about it.

***"In their hearts humans plan their course, but the LORD establishes their steps."***
***~Proverbs 16:9~***

# Kevin Herrick

## -7-
# Peace Before The Storm: Let The Work Begin

Each meeting, the M.U.C. begin by gathering in a common area about fifteen minutes prior to the hard-start time. Before the work night, each guy has an opportunity to hear or see what the workload looks like for the week. That is accomplished via a weekly email, Facebook post, or a "Housekeeping moment" before the start of the previous week's study night. This gathering provides an opportunity to make sure the men are mentally prepared, which is almost as invaluable as being physically ready.

At the start of the work night, the guys will all meet and wait for assignments to be passed out. As the leader and orchestrator of the night's workload, it's my responsibility to match guys up for the tasks at hand. I've made it a practice that the guys are always teamed up with at least one other man (as stated in the last section). A work night is as much as working on relationships as working on the projects themselves. Also, the concept of "two heads are better than one" always stands true.

I've seen where the guys feed off each other to devise viable solutions for whatever the challenge might be. It's essential to understand how many men it will take for each task in order to make everything flow smoothly for the evening.

Ultimately, the more the project ideas of structure and design are explained to the men, the more the men are prepared to succeed. I also believe in empowering and letting each man or group of men start their assigned project independently. Then throughout the work night, I will follow up with each group and direct or redirect them as needed.

Often, I've thought about how convenient it would be to have a scooter or even roller skates so that I can quickly make rounds with each group. Our biggest downfall is that we don't take enough time at the night's end to completely clean the areas we worked in. Occasionally it looks like a storm went through the building, which inevitably means that I'll need to spend a portion of my day on Tuesday cleaning up what didn't get done.

If your structure isn't set up like ours (I'm employed by the church), it may mean spending additional time cleaning up at the end of the night or possibly having one of your groups assigned to help clean up afterward.

One of my most important tasks is to serve the men during work nights. I will bring them water to keep them hydrated and screws if they're out of screws. If they need an extension cord, I'll find one. I do whatever it takes to keep the guys moving and honor their time and commitment.

**So What?**

I will go home completely exhausted at the end of a work night. But also mentally charged because of the amount of work accomplished and the fun we shared as we tackled these projects together.

*"Therefore, my beloved brothers, be steadfast, immovable, always abounding in the work of the Lord, knowing that in the Lord your labor is not in vain."*
*~1 Corinthians 15:58 ESV~*

## It's All About The Bacon

## -8-
# Work Nights: Knowing When To Call It

The nights were going great, with lots of guys showing up. All the projects on your list are in some state of progress. You're bouncing back and forth, ensuring all the guys have everything they need for a win. This activity is a typical work night for us. However, occasionally problems or something unforeseen happens.

I remember years ago when we were doing a major remodel of our sanctuary at our main church campus. Part of the project was to get all the pieces to flow by adding a second-floor entrance to the right side of the backstage. Knowing that this remodel would take multiple work nights, we laid the project out in three work night stages. The other scheduling change we made to keep the Worship Center functioning without canceling church services was to do all three work nights on back-to-back-to-back Monday nights.

We built the staircase during week number two. When we got down to the third and last work night, our final task was to cut an opening in a cinderblock wall on the recently built second-floor staircase and landing. So, one of the guys, Howie, shows up with his gas-powered concrete saw, and the fun begins.

Since we were on the second floor and the rest of the remodel was nearly finished, we couldn't use a wet saw that would coat everything with a layer of wet sludge. So, Howie fired up his saw, and in no time, it looked like an early Midwest Fall morning because the fog was so thick that you couldn't see your hand in front of your face. After 20 minutes of sawing, the hole was cut. However, everything in the Worship Center was coated with a thick layer of concrete dust. The poor guy doing the cutting looked like a dirty ghost, and the only feature of his that had any color was his eyes, and that was only when he would blink. When I looked into his eyes, I saw that "Don't ever ask me to do this again" look. We still talk about that to this day.

## So What?

First, understand your limitations and know when the job may be too messy, dangerous, or time-consuming. In the case of this story, cutting the hole was way messier than we thought it would be. Looking back, we should have hired a professional concrete hole-cutting company with the right saws and a commercial water recovery system. I feel that I may have burned up some good favor with the guys at that time. Thankfully, they gave me grace and saw the big picture and the project's ultimate success. Praise The Lord! The project got done on time and within budget.

## -9-
# Providing Dessert And Fellowship

Whether you're having a work or study night, having dessert afterward is imperative. It took me over a year to realize how important a simple dessert could be. I wasn't fully aware until one of the spouses approached me and offered to make a dessert for each of our MUC events. Once we got used to having dessert and fellowship time, there was no turning back. The dessert portion of an evening meeting provided a time for the men to talk outside of an organized structure. I quickly learned that this dessert and fellowship time should be largely unstructured to foster an informal atmosphere. What I've found that works well is to inform the group at the beginning of the event what kind of dessert we'll be having once the event is concluded. By doing this, a level of anticipation can be established to help keep some of the guys attentive, thus getting more men to hang out longer and get to know each other better while building stronger long-term relationships.

Where does all this dessert come from? Besides the story at the end of this chapter, these desserts have ranged from guys picking up cookies at the local bakery and asking some of the spouses to make a cake or two to me making cakes an hour prior to the meeting. Whatever it takes to provide a great experience, we do it.

One of the most popular desserts we've had is what we call a "dump cake." Honestly, I had never heard of a dump cake until 15 years ago when a cherry-white dump cake was made by one of the spouses. It is a simple cake to make and well received by all the guys. This cake is so simple that now it's my "go-to" dessert when I'm pressed for time and no one else has offered to bring something.

Here's how it goes: Take a can of pie filling (cherry, apple, blueberries, or raspberry), throw it in an 11'x'13' greased pan, and spread it evenly. Next, take a can of shredded pineapple (non-drained) and lay that on top of the pie filling. Finally, sprinkle a cake mix (white, yellow, chocolate) over the pie filling and the crushed pineapple mix, spreading it out as evenly as possible. Then, pour a stick of melted butter over the cake mix. Place into the oven @ 350 degrees for 20 minutes or until the cake mix is lightly browned.

The final and most important aspect of the dessert time is that the leader should be the server. There's nothing better than serving your volunteers and letting them know they are genuinely appreciated. Our very first volunteer for desserts was Carol. Carol saw a need and answered the call.

## Carol's Story-

When Ernie (my husband) was about 64 years old, he informed me he was joining a new men's group at church. I was somewhat surprised this was coming from a man who had never had any desire to join any sort of group previously, especially not a church group. This group had a two-fold agenda.

The first Monday night would be a work night around the church, and the following Monday night was a Bible study night designed just for the men. Ernie has always loved working with his hands, so I wasn't surprised why the work night appealed to him, but I was unsure about the Bible study part.

After the first work night, Ernie came home excited about what they had accomplished. He literally couldn't stop talking about their night. Imagine my surprise as this was "my husband," who barely ever spoke about anything. However, the next time these guys would get together would be for the Bible study, and I questioned if he would like it. Well, to my surprise, he sure did.

Although he didn't have as much to say about it as he did on the work night, as time went on, Ernie got more and more excited about this group and started inviting every man he met.

I saw their work and felt his excitement continue every week, even though he was often very hungry and tired when he came home from work nights. I asked him if anyone thought about bringing a dessert for the time after the work or study was done. Of course, he replied that they were so busy that no one could take the time to stop and eat. So, I decided to contact the leader (Kevin) and let him know that I would be willing to provide some sort of dessert for the guys after every Monday night that they would meet (either work or study night). Kevin said, "Yes, let's give it a try."

I honestly think Ernie has enjoyed the desserts as much, if not more, than the other guys! I had no idea how much I would enjoy baking for these hard-working men. His communication about all that was happening in this group became a huge blessing to me. Even though the guy's motto was "What's said at M.U.C. stays at M.U.C.," Ernie would still share with me what the guys would say about the desserts I provided and how much these sweet treats were appreciated. The guys were always so generous with their compliments. I came to know who liked what and which dessert was everyone's favorite.

I would often make a cherry "dump cake." I was never really sure, but Ernie said it was one of the guys' favorite desserts.

After a few years of making desserts every Monday night, I decided it was time to pass the torch on to some of the other spouses, so they could receive the same joy I did through baking for the men. I still bake some, just not as often.

Now there are so many other creative wives that love to bake, represented in the group, and the men always appreciate whatever desserts they have for their fellowship time. I once heard, "There's nothing a dessert can't fix," and I say, "Desserts should never be eaten alone." These guys from Men Under Construction are living proof that these two sayings are spot on.

*"So whether you eat or drink, or whatever you do, do it all for the glory of God."*
*~1 Corinthians 10:31~*

## -10-
# Having Good Spiritual Tools In Your Toolbox

Even if it's not a study night, we have realized there should still be an opportunity for each man to somehow engage spiritually at any MUC event. It is awesome to see how guys interact with each other while they are working side by side on work nights, especially when the work is for the growth of the Kingdom. I've witnessed firsthand the level of vulnerability that the men share when they know that their work can somehow impact the lives of the congregation. It seems that every aspect of a MUC gathering can become a moment of growth and spiritual awakening.

I must admit that sharing a meaningful story or lesson on work nights isn't always possible. However, we do try to take a few minutes to capture the good things that are going on in our church community.

We have started referring to some of these moments as using the tools from our "Spiritual Toolbox." Some of the utensils in our Spiritual Toolbox that help make connections on non-study nights would be scripture memorized by the guys, daily devotional books with short two-to-three-minute stories, and real-life application anecdotes that the guys are willing to share. We've learned that the best time to share these stories or short scripture lessons is during dessert and fellowship time.

Some of the noteworthy contributors to our MUC conversations include Bob, who is notorious for spouting off scripture that hits the nail on the head each time; Jerry, who is excellent at sharing short stories that really make one think; and Don, who has many stories about the struggles in his life and how he has overcome them, or how being a part of MUC has given him a better outlook on life. It's fairly easy for any of the guys to share a life story or a testimony that's uplifting and beneficial, especially when it's short and unstructured.

**So What?**

These unstructured conversations make a significant impact on the men. Setting up a time such as this is ideal for any of the men to take the lead and run with it. They don't have to be leaders or teachers. All they need to do is have a voice and a story. Sharing stories during this time helps the guys learn more about each other, and at the same time, it can help the presenter feel more comfortable as well.

*"Iron sharpens iron, and one man sharpens another."*
*~Proverbs 27:17 ESV~*

## -11-
# Each Man Has Something To Offer

When the work night is getting wrapped up, and the projects have been declared either finished or to a level of completion that can be called quits, the guys all know to collect themselves back at the starting point, where desserts are being served. This closing time is also when we can have a bit of a devotion or hear a life story from one of the guys. In addition, having the guys together for a few moments is also a great time to throw out questions about how their projects went. Sometimes you'll get a positive response, sometimes not.

During this time, the leader should present a positive attitude regardless of how the night went. Always remember that these men freely give their time and talents to see projects around the church completed and to take pressure off the maintenance staff and the church budget. So, take the time to acknowledge your appreciation and convey that without them, many things simply wouldn't get done. Remember that these work nights create sustainability and allow the church's financial resources to go more toward ministry and less toward maintenance.

Several of the MUC guys really helped us realize that each man has something unique to offer. Here are the stories of a few of those men.

**Leonard's Story-
A Guy with a Huge Heart**

Leonard was one of the original 12 guys who answered the call to start the new men's group. The first time I met him, I saw this frail old man (he was 82 at the time), and my initial thought was, "Great, I'm going to have to keep my eye on this old man to make sure he doesn't get hurt or kick the bucket." Leonard had spent the previous year facing a severe bout with depression. His depression was so bad that he would sit in a dark room, in a dark corner, and just stare at nothingness. Leonard had also suffered a heart attack two years prior to joining us. He felt his life was effectively over, and he simply wanted God to take him away. His cardiologist told Leonard that only 10% of his heart was functioning.

Leonard had always been a self-made man with a strong-spirited wife and great kids. But since his heart attack, he felt he was worthless and a burden to his family. Somehow his daughter convinced him to give the new men's group a try and see if it was something that would fit him.

Well, Leonard and the other MUC guys hit it off wonderfully. Even though everyone could see how frail Leonard was, the guys still saw him as a whole man with a pleasant smile and a desire to seek meaning in what he felt was left of his life. Over the years, we all learned so much from Leonard. On work nights, he would always be there, even though all he could do was push a broom or offer a word of encouragement.

We all especially gleaned so much from Leonard on the study nights. Primarily because of his life experiences, he gave us a glimpse into the life of someone who faced overpowering physical challenges and mental depression.

After about a year of being a "MUC guy," Leonard came to me and asked if he could volunteer four hours a day at the church doing anything that would benefit us. We discovered that although he was slow and meticulous,

Leonard had a great passion for organization. He spent the next two years as a solid and reliable church volunteer.

We took an old, out-of-the-way storage closet and let Leonard go to town on it. He organized all our tools and supplies in that space, and now the MUC men are much more productive.

Even though Leonard has been gone for 13 years, we still call our tool storage area "Leonard's closet." Each year during our MUC anniversary celebration, when we talk about our brothers that have passed, Leonard is still honored. He is known as the guy who felt he had nothing to offer and yet turned into the best example of commitment and perseverance we have ever seen.

**So What?**

Every man has something to offer to the group. Ultimately, Leonard's most significant attribute was his loyalty and commitment.

Learn to empower the men God puts in your path and keep an open mind to see where the Holy Spirit leads them. Many men will say something like, "I'm not handy, so I don't think this group is a good fit for me." Although it might take some convincing and assuring to get past that stigma, it is well worth the effort. The following story is about a guy who falls into that category.

**Mike's Story-**
**The Guy Who Found the Skill**

Mike joined our MUC group sometime around 2010. He's a tall guy with strong stature. For his career of choice, Mike drove for FedEx up to his retirement. Mike has a gift for remembering facts and details about many things and can recall moments from many years ago with great accuracy. Mike would be there for all the MUC study nights and most work nights.

He was a good fit when it came time to partner him up with the other more skilled men for the work nights. We would continually strive to team up talent with potential talent. The point here is that Mike was always a potential talent. For a guy who could talk to anyone about anything, Mike lacked the confidence to tackle any sizable construction project on his own. But he continued to watch and learn, taking note of the successes and learning from the other guys who really got it.

Occasionally, Mike would get teamed up with another guy who would inspire and challenge him to learn and grow in understanding construction processes. Mike came to me a while back, and he was very excited. Mike had decided to tackle a major remodel at his house all by himself. The project was a major bathroom retrofit. I can't say that Mike didn't run into any challenging issues, we all have them, but Mike said he gained enough confidence from all his years of work night experience that he knew he was ready. Afterward, I saw his completed project, and all I could say was, "Congratulations Mike." His handy work, albeit complex, was completed to a very high standard.

## So What?

Over the years we have had Men Under Construction, I've seen this same dynamic, such as Mike, happen multiple times. It is incredibly rewarding to see how well the partnerships and learning experiences forged during the work nights can blossom and produce a more confident soul.

**Billy's Story-
Our Cross Man**

Another one of the long-standing members of MUC is Billy, otherwise known as the "Cross Man." Billy is always a source of encouragement and one of the guys you can count on when you need help with almost any task. Billy often refers to himself as a "Man Under Construction," He has recruited several men to join or return to the group over the years. One of Billy's passions is making wooden crosses. He has made crosses for literally thousands of people, including extra-large ones for other ministries, all for free. Today there are people worldwide wearing one of his crosses that, according to him, "God made, and he just cut them out." On a couple of work nights, the MUC men helped cut out or sand and prepared hundreds of crosses to be handed out during baptisms.

**So What?**

Guys like Leonard, Mike, and Billy, as well as the many other "all-in" MUC men, help make it a joy to have this MUC group. Seeing all the fruit of all the excellent work they have done is truly inspirational.

*"He who began a good work in you will carry it on to completion until the day of Christ Jesus."
~Philippians 1:6~*

## -12-
# Our M.U.C. Policy:
# Keeping All Work At Heritage Properties

When we first started doing the work night portion of MUC, the question of doing projects off-site came up. I must admit that I struggled with this question for quite a while. On the one hand, we had many opportunities to build, repair or destroy stuff on the church's premises. However, there is always a need for willing volunteers to help those in the community who sometimes don't have the means to help themselves. We decided our answer to this question via prayer and consensus. Fortunately, a couple of guys were very familiar with Habitat for Humanity and how they are structured. They gave the group several stories of their work and how intense it sometimes could get. There were multiple aspects to be aware of, such as insurance liability, which covers poor workmanship, and what happens if someone gets injured while working on a non-church-owned property. I threw my concerns to the group one night before our next MUC work night. Based on everything we learned and the desire not to get overwhelmed by outside requests, we chose to keep all work nights focused on church-only projects, with the exemption of an occasional international church-building mission venture.

Over the years, we have had a decent share of international missions' projects. The MUC guys have been blessed to be able to travel to work on projects established through our church in such places as Russia, Ecuador, Haiti, and Africa. Most of our projects thus far have been in Haiti, where we have been asked to build or rebuild churches in difficult construction situations. Many of these projects have required specialty teams highly skilled at problem-solving and can work incredibly well in unconventional conditions, which is what MUC does best.

Here is an example of how one of our MUC guys used his God-given skills to pull off a remarkable feat of engineering.

**Eric's Story-
Was it Luck?**

On one of our four trips to Haiti, we were tasked to rebuild churches destroyed by the 2010 earthquakes. A longtime MUC guy named Eric was asked to figure out what it would take to complete a parsonage in Jacmel. The catch was that the rebuilding of the parsonage had been started a year earlier by locals, who eventually gave up hope of completing the project since the roof rafters were going to be unusually complicated with multiple hinge points and complex overhangs. Eric was soon to be a retired mechanical engineer from a well-known animal food producer. Eric's specialty was figuring out how to deliver a food product from beginning to end and all the assembly processes in between. Eric was a great asset to MUC and brought strategy and organization to several Christmas and Easter prop projects. Especially those props that required some sort of mechanical ingenuity.

Eric loved the challenge of the Haiti project and wouldn't let this one pass him by. He took a 2011 Google map aerial view of the uncompleted parsonage, copied it, blew it up, and then digitally laid it out so he could do his best to measure the walls and their distances from each other. By the time we got to Haiti, Eric had a complete set of roof rafter prints, which were ready to be built. So, the day came for Eric to test his planning and intuition with the reality on the ground. It was like we were witnessing a miracle in real time. From the height of 12,700 miles in the sky, Eric had nailed it within one inch of perfection. His connection points were spot on, and his overhangs were perfect. Eric and his fellow MUC guys who worked on this project were "on cloud nine" for the whole week. Still, to this day, you can see that special twinkle in Eric's eye when he talks about that miraculous opportunity.

## So What?

Like Eric, there are so many men out there who have great ideas. Your responsibility as a leader is to help the men identify their gifts and talents and to set them free to come up with solutions.

It will be amazing for you to witness what the Holy Spirit does with willing men who link arms together for His purpose and glory.

***"Unless the LORD builds the house, its builders labor in vain."***
***~ Psalm 127~***

# Kevin Herrick

## It's All About The Bacon

## -13-
# Props, Props, And More Props

Over the years, we have had hundreds of projects that we needed to design and build. Out of all these opportunities to build something, the most rewarding items have always been building stage props. I think the reason why we all enjoy making stage props is two-fold. Not only does it provide us a means to be incredibly creative, but we were also able to see these props in action and witness how the community interacted with each of these wonderful fabrications. Several of our prop creations get referenced often when the MUC guys get together. In many ways, these props and projects have defined who we are. They are creative, thoughtful, challenging, and even somewhat mystical (kind of like "pay no attention to that man behind the curtain").

Besides benefiting our church, we also feel the design, construction, and implementation work we do is our way of ministering to our community. Some props we created were used in venues that ministered to the local community. What follows are a few thoughts from Scott Schaefer, the Worship Pastor and Executive Director of our Creative Christmas program.

**Scott Schaefer's Letter**

In all my years at Heritage church, it has been an honor to work with so many talented and gifted men in Men Under Construction. Not only did they offer their services materially but spiritually as well. During the Creative Christmas days, there were many times when I thought things simply could not have been built, but I never forgot about the passion of the MUC guys and how they could pretty much make anything happen. There was a time during the early morning hours when the men constructed stages and props that fulfilled the vision of the show. I remember literally laying on my back, holding things in place as they built a rather LARGE oval walkway for one of the shows. It was about 2 am, and they were still at it. Funny, but I had a great time getting to know several of the guys while I was lying on my back holding things in place.

As I reflect over the years, I have gotten many positive comments about the show as the producer, and I firmly believe that the shows would not have been as successful as they were if not for the tireless efforts of the MUC guys. For that, I'm forever thankful to Kevin and the guys. They should have gotten as much credit as we all did who were on the stage, and if not, I want to give it to them now, "Thanks, guys, for making an eternal difference in people's lives!"

*Scott Schaefer, Former Worship Leader*

The name of this book is "It's All About the Bacon," and every man loves bacon. Besides the task of rendering that delicious pork, the MUC men also love working on the props. We've created props for Christmas shows, Easter Celebrations, Good Friday events, the Children's department, and several special sermon series. I've included several stories or descriptions of these prop projects in order to capture your attention and perhaps help open your eyes to the potential fun things you might do as a group. The first story below is from Ron. Ron is an engineer who thrives on tough challenges. Hopefully, you also have a "Ron" in your men's group.

## Ron's Stories-
## Charlie Brown's Christmas Tree

One of the challenges the MUC men were given was to create a skimpy little Christmas tree like the one in the beloved Charlie Brown Christmas Story. If you remember, as soon as Charlie Brown tried to decorate this tree, the needles fell off, and all he was left with was an even skimpier tree. So, our task was to make a prop resembling his poor excuse for a Christmas tree. Adding to the challenge was the requirement that the tree would be used in a half dozen Creative Christmas shows, and it would have to be reset up reasonably quickly. Knowing the expectations and being someone who works primarily in metal, I put my thinking cap on and waited for my old brain to generate some creative and unique ideas.

I started with Aluminum conduit because I had used aluminum electrical conduit for projects before and knew that although it is rigid, it is still easy to bend. I started with a larger size conduit for the tree trunk (three inches in diameter) and welded on progressively smaller diameters as I worked my way up, creating the branches. At the end of the branches, I used a two-inch ring of thin steel conduit that would slide over the aluminum conduit making up the tips of the branches. These sliding steel sleeves were actuated with small steel cables that slipped inside the branches and then worked their way down the trunk. The cables all joined together within the last bottom section of the conduit. Then the line went out the bottom of the tree, through the cross-shaped wood base, and finally under the stage, where a crew member would pull the cable at the right moment to drop the needles from the end of the branches. The needles were made of painted green electrical wire with the twelve-gauge copper ends flattened out to friction fit in between the aluminum "branches" and the sliding steel sleeves.

Ten pieces of wire were pushed into the area between the thin sleeve and the conduit that made up the tip of the Charlie Brown tree. When the sleeves were pulled (via the wire going through the tree), the needles fell off to the ground, just like what Linus experienced when he then wrapped his blue blanket around the base of the tree.

A few other MUC members added their artistic touch by using filler material and paint to add texture and color to the aluminum frame to make it look more like natural tree bark. The sound of the painted copper needles, along with a few keystrokes from a piano, made for a very believable "tinkle" sound as the wires hit the hard surface of the stage. As I remember, the tree worked flawlessly throughout the multiple shows. Thankfully, I recall hearing many "How did they do that?" comments from the crowd.

## The Street Scene

The largest task I recall we did at our church property was building a complete street scene for a Christmas production. The scene required three full-size buildings (Hardware store, house, and duplex), along with a 1968 Volkswagen that puttered out puffs of exhaust. The set also needed streetlights, falling snow and even two teenage drummers lowered from the ceiling rafters while playing the beginning of the Christmas standard "Drummer Boy."

The houses were basic wood structures with vinyl siding (found on Facebook Marketplace second-hand). We used basic construction practices for the windows and doors (also second-hand items). These props were heavy and hard to move, but since we didn't need to move them very far, we could get away with overbuilding everything. The scene was so fun to build because once we finished the basics for the buildings, it didn't take much else to make it feel real. We placed lamps in the windows, used roof shingles made of cardboard (to keep the weight down), and a fog machine that hazed over the scene to present a feeling of Winter. We borrowed a full-size True Value hardware sign for the exterior of our Hardware store. We placed ladders and wheelbarrows in the store's windows and lightly backlit these areas. It looked real and wonderful.

It's All About The Bacon

**Easter Story Book**

The easiest and most effective prop we ever did was during an eight-week Easter sermon series. We found a company that rented out backdrops in all sorts of sizes. Our main stage is 20 feet tall by 40 feet wide. We found a backdrop that had a very fairytale-ish feeling to it. All we needed to do then to create the desired atmosphere was add a few three-dimensional props, and we were set.

We built three 2-foot wide by 24-foot-tall tree trunks out of concrete footing forms. We used two-by-four lumber inside of the tubes to give them structure and then used spray foam on the exterior of the tubes in order to replicate the bark. The final step was to use a Paper Mache mixture of newspaper and flour to wrap the tubes, followed by a simple three-tone paint job. Once these basics were done, we built three 4-foot by 4-foot houses using scrap lumber and fake brick siding for the "Three Little Pigs" sermon. The cool thing about these little houses is that when the Pastor went up and physically blew on them, the sides of the houses fell outward. It's amazing what can be done with fishing wire, spring hinges, and pulleys.

For the Wizard of Oz set, we first bought a life-size cut out of the Tin Man. We then built a yellow brick road using cheap Masonite brick paneling and painted a light coat of safety yellow paint over the top of the bricks. I thought it looked pretty convincing. I wish we had thrown in some flying monkeys, too, because I know we have a few MUC guys who would have willingly jumped on that opportunity!

**The Six Elves with Confetti Guns**

We love goofing around at MUC, and whenever we get a chance to show off our creative, fun-loving side, we'll jump all over it. One of the funniest shenanigans involving hand-held props that we ever did was during a Christmas Eve service at our main church campus. We started by figuring out how t-shirt launchers were built.

Once we established that these launchers used momentary on-switches, compressed air, and a nine-volt pulse trigger, we designed and built our own version, understanding that these launchers would need to shoot a pound of confetti 50-60' in the air. The unit would need to be entirely self-contained.

Surprisingly we found everything we needed at our local Menards store. We spent one work night building the prototype and the next testing the "confetti launcher." Once we knew we had a workable version, we set out to build eight additional launchers. The launcher consisted of an air tank with a Schrader valve, a heavy-duty lawn sprinkler shut-off valve, a high-volume air pressure gauge, a nine-volt battery, the trigger, and of course, the barrel that was large enough to hold a pound of confetti. After we assembled each launcher, we applied a coat of white paint followed by a red candy-striped band from top to bottom.

On the night of "the show," six of the MUC guys (dressed in red plaid and Santa hats) quickly marched into the middle of the Worship Center, drew their launchers 45 degrees, and spewed 6 pounds of half-inch confetti over everyone who was enjoying the service that night. We did this four times that night! The floor of the Worship Center was utterly covered with snow-white confetti, and of course, we had the pleasure of vacuuming it all up afterward.

## The I-74 bridge mock-up for our 40th Anniversary

Our community is divided by the Mighty Mississippi River. The river has always presented a considerable issue whenever there's an attempt to get both sides of the river's communities together. Our main campus is located in Illinois, while our second campus is five miles away, just across the Mississippi River. There is a bridge between both communities known as the I-74 bridge. A troll lives under the bridge and is known for creating havoc on that bridge, often at rush hour. Not really, but the bridge is old and narrow, with no place to pull off if there is an accident or a stalled car. The bridge was built in the 1940s, with a second section added in the 1950s. Nonetheless, this bridge has created quite a chasm between the folks in Iowa and Illinois.

In April 2015, we were asked to build a fifty-foot version of our I-74 bridge for our church's 50th Anniversary celebration. The idea was to have the Senior Pastor preaching from the bridge's deck. His sermon was about the bridge and how it divided our two communities for many years. However, the church is building a bridge connecting our two communities through the power and might of the Holy Spirit. For the record, a new I-74 bridge was finally constructed and finished in 2021.

To build our bridge replica, we needed sturdy steel supports that could tower twenty-two feet tall and support a deck (simulation of the road) and all the suspension cables since the original I-74 bridge was a suspension bridge. One of our MUC guys had several pieces of pallet racking that we could use, which were perfect for the project. It took us four work nights to build the entire structure. We mocked it up so well that we even had working air traffic lights on top of the towers and an owl statue perched next to the lights to keep the pigeons off the cables, just like the original.

The prop was fifty-eight feet long, four-foot-wide and twenty-two feet tall. There were two identical spans complete with traffic striping and suspension cables holding it all up. The pastor entered "the bridge" via an on-ramp on one side. Since this event would be larger than any of our buildings could handle, we rented a local ten-thousand-seat venue. We then needed to disassemble our bridge, load it up on a semi-trailer and haul it three miles away to the venue. It was quite a sight watching it go down the road.

## It's All About The Bacon

## The Tree on Top of the Tower

In 2017 we purchased a large piece of property that was iconic in the Quad Cities. It included a 180-foot-tall tower where the previous owner would place a 30-foot-tall real Christmas tree on top every December since the early 1970s. So, once we purchased the property, the number one question we would be asked was, "Are you putting the tree back up this year?" The previous trees on the tower were placed with an elaborate foldable crane permanently attached to the roof. During the years that they set a real tree on the tower, two of the trees had snapped in half and had to be sawed up and precariously loaded into an elevator to get back to ground level. I thought this was ridiculously risky, and it seemed a better plan could be implemented. So, we MUC guys got together and brainstormed for a better idea. What we came up with was completely sustainable and a whole lot safer.

First, the original real trees were whittled down to fit into a flagpole holder that was erected into the roof structure. We found a 30-foot aluminum flagpole and hoisted it into place on top of the roof using the old crane. Next, we worked with a local HVAC company to roll two-inch stainless-steel slats into fourteen separate circles. The top circle was two feet in diameter, and the bottom ring was fifteen feet in diameter. We also fastened a one-foot aluminum plate to the top of the pole. This top plate had four pulley rollers bolted on top of itself. These rollers allowed us to feed quarter-inch stainless steel aircraft cable from the bottom of the flagpole to the rollers and then back to the rooftop.

The rings were then bolted onto the stainless-steel cable at two-foot increments. Finally, we used four basic "boat winches" bolted to the flagpole's base to lift the new ring-style Christmas tree up and into its resting place.

We used 180 strands of icicle lights that were zip-tied in place to light each of these fourteen rings. We wrapped two passes of icicle lights on each circle to get the brightness and effect we wanted. Altogether, there were 18,000 lights. Finally, a star needed to be placed on top. So, we built a four-foot-tall diamond shape out of two-inch aluminum tubing and fastened multicolored LED light strips to the outside edge of the aluminum pipes. We then attached the star to a thirty-foot aluminum pipe and set it alongside the flagpole up the middle of the rings. It was beautiful and just as big and bright as the previous Christmas trees.

Doing all this was satisfying because we carried on a tradition in our community that was so badly missed and appreciated. There was a seven-year gap when nothing was done on the tower for multiple reasons. But now it was all good, and our community once again enjoyed the spirit of Christmas together.

It's All About The Bacon

**Drummer Boy**

If you have ever seen the Blue Man Group or the rhythmic group STOMP, you would know how fun and entertaining they can be. We were asked to incorporate the Blue Man Group and STOMP-like dynamics into our final production during our Creative Christmas production. Usually, at the end of our Christmas show, the church band and the youth group would perform a lively rendition of the old standard "Drummer Boy." Over the twenty years, I was involved with the program, we had so many different interesting variations, but this one was the most challenging and unique by far. Keep in mind that each of these unique props (or musical instruments) took hours of trial and error to perfect the desired effect.

One of the craziest rhythmic props we needed to build was a "Wall of Percussion." It was a ten-foot high by a twenty-foot-wide steel frame with heavy wire mesh welded onto it. This wall needed to be freestanding while still supporting a few people climbing all over the surface of it. The next task was to find the required "junk" to attach to the screen. This junk needed to produce a particular sound when struck with a drumstick or a hammer. We gathered propane tanks, old steam radiators, steel truck rims, muffler pipes, glass jars, bottles, garbage can lids, plastic five-gallon buckets, and other clunky odds and ends. Once we laid out all the pieces on the wall, we had to figure out how to attach each piece so that the "instrument" could be struck multiple times without falling off. We needed to maintain sound integrity as well.

Now that everything was in place on the wall, we attached heavy chains to the top and flew it about ten feet off the stage deck. Our portion of this prop was then completed. On the night of the show, three people would be hung by body harnesses in front of the wall. Fifty-foot cables suspended these musicians from the venue's ceiling, allowing them room to swing around and play whatever instrument they needed to strike to create the "Drummer" portion of the song. And to use a pun, it was a huge hit!

During several other years, when the Drummer Boy finale was performed, we would use drums known as "Floor Toms" to create the required sound and rhythmic effect. The first year was simple. We built a quantity of three ten-foot-long wooden trays that were about five inches tall and mounted to some really smooth rolling casters. We then fastened four Floor Toms into each rolling tray. Next, we wired flood lights to the bottom of the tray, one for each Floor Tom, and then placed colored film (known as gels) under the head or skin of the Floor Toms and installed triggers into each. These triggers picked up every hit of a drumstick and would turn on the spotlight momentarily via some other fancy controls. These were cool and functional, but we couldn't help but up our game over the next few years. As the Floor Toms design progressed, we waterproofed the rolling trays, added a small water pump and water supply to each drum, installed some hidden plumbing from the water pumps to the top of the drums, and warned the kids (the drummers) that they should expect to get soaked by the end of the production. Needless to say, it was quite a splash! Whenever the drumhead was struck with a drumstick, the water flowing across the head would bounce at least a few feet upward.

The water would catch the color from the light and gel, making it look like paint splashed all over. Eventually, we switched to color-changing LED lights, giving us even more creative options.

Throughout the years that the Creative Christmas production ran, we went through dozens of garbage cans and lids, Marching Toms, PVC tubing, and drumsticks to keep the performances going. But one of the most challenging Drummer Boy projects was the year that the Worship Arts department decided to use different sizes and shapes of bottles to produce the sounds they wanted. Furthermore, to make things a bit more interesting, they wanted everything lit using black lights! Our first step was to figure out what to fill the bottles with to catch the black lighting.

Thankfully one of our guys had some experience with this (how and why, not really sure). By his instruction, we filled the containers with tonic water. Apparently, tonic water contains quinine, which absorbs and reflects the black lighting rather well.

Our next task was to figure out how to mount these various-sized bottles and glass containers to some sort of frame that wouldn't hinder the sound of the glass once it was struck with a drumstick. We devised a really cool wooden box-style frame that held each container in suspension using heavy filament string. We needed six of these frames to cover the stage entirely. The next and final process was to establish how to light the frame with black lights without obstructing the view from the audience. Once all the pieces were in place, we attached a square glass container to the front of each drummer. Doing this created a much livelier effect since the drummers were hardly ever seen (unless they smiled), but now with the lit glass container attached to the front of them, it was easy to see how they moved and drummed with the beat. It was a blessed challenge, and the MUC guys loved to oblige.

**So What?**

Prop design and construction are a blast. Building props allows us to show off our God-given skills and raise the production quality of our sermons and performances. Personally, I love the complexity of these props and how the problem-solving process can draw so many of the men together to discover a solution and thus create a sense of great accomplishment.

It's All About The Bacon

**"Without consultation and wise advice, plans are frustrated, But with many counselors they are established and succeed."**
*~Proverbs 15:22 AMP~*

## -14-
# Study Night Structure: Well, Sort Of

Since 2004, our study night structure has remained pretty much the same. We have recently moved our start time up a half an hour to allow for more post-fellowship time. Here's what a study night generally looks like. The leader gets there at least 30 minutes prior, during which time they are setting up tables and chairs for the fellowship and dessert after study time. Guys start arriving and typically start right in with fellowship. I've observed where the men will initially gather around the tables, not necessarily in organized groups or even in groups where everyone is well known. Occasionally, I'll use this table time to throw out a thought-provoking question to get the night going in the right direction. I generally start with an opening phrase like "Around your table." We then call the group to move to the circle (we most always sit in a circle). I have found that our communications are best when everyone can see each other, and everyone can be seen. Sitting in a circle has its challenges, especially if you're in a smaller building. But the benefits greatly outweigh the challenges. As the leader in the circle, I can easily see everyone's facial expressions and pretty much tell if someone is having difficulty following along with the subject.

The next step is to do a bit of "Housekeeping." I'll spend a few minutes discussing the upcoming work night and give a list of the potential projects. This period is also the best time to discuss future group events. On a few occasions, we immediately started discussing the previous day's main church sermon message. It is incredible to witness when your church happens to be in step with the topic of discussion that night, or vice-versa. This discussion time occurs quite frequently. Ultimately, the leader must be in tune with what The Holy Spirit is prodding, as it makes all the difference. Then someone will open with a simple prayer asking the Holy Spirit to open our ears, minds, and hearts to what He wants us to receive. Then we dive into the night's study topic.

If everything goes well, we finish the study within an hour, which leaves us enough time for some group "one-on-one" time. The one-on-one time often presents the best opportunity for transparency and allows the men to express life change. I will typically start with the guy directly across the circle from me. I'll ask, "How are you doing? What can we pray for?" Depending on the group size, the amount of time available, and the intensity in the room, I may stipulate that it's okay just to say, "I'm good," and move on to the next guy.

Through this exercise, I have experienced such a wonderful amount of wisdom from The Holy Spirit about each man and what's truly going on in their life. Having this insightful gift frequently makes the evening interesting. Sometimes I will intentionally call something out that the Holy Spirit is "whispering" in my ear about a situation or a hurt. Being in tune with God's Spirit and willing to be wrong makes an excellent setup for honest and genuine healing moments.

Once in a while, a situation will come up where one of the guys is really hurting. This trauma can mean physical, emotional, or spiritual suffering and frequently a combination of hurtful dynamics. With little apology or fanfare, one of the guys will grab a chair from the stack and set it up in the middle of the group circle. We will ALL gather around this hurting brother, place our hands on him (and each other), and pray over him.

One guy in particular often testifies about the moment he ended up in "the chair" with the guys gathered around him, begging God to work in his family's life. John was struggling with clarity. His daughter had been estranged from the family, and nobody knew who was caring for their grandson. The daughter was deeply involved with some bad actors who had recently been busted for drug use and possession. Everything in John's life seemed to be falling apart, except for his strong relationship with his wife.

I vividly remember the prayers brought before God by the MUC men. They asked God for peace, wisdom, guidance, and healing for John and his family.

Praise the Lord, it has been well over ten years since that day, and John's daughter is clean and married to a great guy. Their relationship has never been better. In addition, the grandson is now married and living a good and fruitful life.

Other opportunities that come up during our one-on-one "how are you doing" moments are birthday and anniversary celebrations, retirement celebrations, work situations, and a gamut of other topics. Often, sarcasm will also enter this sacred area, so we all acknowledge that sarcasm must be a spiritual gift because we all seem to possess some of it. Thus, our time isn't always so serious. There is plenty of laughter to go along with the tears. Many nights, I believe I strained a rib from laughing too hard.

Personally, I find it funny that the guys are always picking on my height of 5'8," being follicle challenged, and the fact that I am constantly equipped with my trusty flip flops.

## So What?

The study nights, one-on-ones, and the prayer time that follows allow everyone the opportunity to interact with each other. These are such special and blessed exercises, and the men really appreciate them. These are times when the Holy Spirit can be so evident and present in our lives. There is something special about witnessing the men become passionate about sharing themselves that can truly warm your soul and recharge your spiritual battery.

*"Therefore confess your sins to each other and pray for each other so that you may be healed"*
*~James 5:16~*

## -15-
## Finding The Right Study Topic For The Right Time

Since we started meeting in 2004, we have used over sixty different books for our study time. I have come across and read many great resources over the years. However, the biggest challenge is finding a study relevant to what is happening within the group. Right now, as I am writing this book, I find myself torn between two different studies. One is really deep, with a lot of words and not many questions. The other is based more on scripture and has some good questions. However, it isn't as deep or thought-provoking as the other study.

My library is growing and includes many good study books I haven't decided to use yet, but I will hang on to them for the foreseeable future. You never really know what direction the Holy Spirit will lead the guys in the future or what sort of challenge the group will face. Another consideration that I give to all the study guides is the format. I ask myself about the book, "Is it in the appropriate tone and tenor for our MUC agenda?" When I first started our MUC group, we still had a Christian bookstore in our local community. I found it easy to spend a few hours going through the shelves of Bible studies to see what might work best for our group. Now it is a bit more challenging only using the available online resources. While shopping online, I often thought I had found the perfect study guide until it later arrived, and I discovered the format or interactive portions were not what I had hoped for.

Regarding the study guide format, a few things need to be checked off for it to "click well" with the group. When we meet for our study nights, the guys need to be able to respond to a subject reasonably promptly; otherwise, they may not engage well in the discussion. I have seen the guys get that glazed-over look on their faces when there is just too much to read. The studies that I feel work best are the ones that the author doesn't beat around the bush. The author must get directly to the point.

Another thing I look for in the study material is if it has plenty of thought-provoking questions, either throughout the study or at the end of the chapter. These questions should also be mentally challenging and even somewhat uncomfortable to answer. I frequently find study questions in some guides redundant or irrelevant to the group. Often, I will cross out questions on my copy of the study material in order to reduce some of these less desirable questions, thus leaving more discussion time for the meaty questions.

## Study Examples

We've done two very different studies on Revelation over the past several years. We chose to jump back into Revelation again when everything seemed upside-down due to the pandemic of 2020-2021. There was so much uncertainty in every aspect of life at the time that studying how it's all going to end affirmed that God has it all under control, and He wins.

A study on "The importance of Relationships" seemed necessary when our church underwent a Senior Pastor change. The MUC guys were looking for spiritual guidance they didn't seem to get during the larger weekend services. We've done the book of Romans multiple times over the years since Romans contains the foundation for the Christian walk. I find it amazing how you can read a passage, interpret it one way, reread it a few years later, and discover a whole new meaning. I remember when we did a study on the book of James. The first chapter is so impactful, and it gave the guys something they could relate to and claim as promises God made directly to them. All in all, we've pretty much covered the entire New Testament.

One of the most impactful studies I recall was "Telling my story." The idea behind this study was to help each man develop their own testimony and to be able to present a two to three-minute version of it to share with others. At the end of this study, we set up a night where three guys could share their stories with the group.

Of course, we set the meeting up in a large circle, and then we had a table and two chairs in the center of the group. The conversation starter was, Imagine you're at a coffee house and run into an old friend. The conversation grows to where you can give your testimony as a witness to what's going on in your life. The first two guys did a great job. I was really proud of their effort.

The third guy who gave his testimony during the night was breathtakingly awesome. This fellow's name was Tom, and he was a member of a local biker's club. His position in the club was that of "an enforcer." Therefore, he was charged to ensure the members kept the rules and to dish out punishment to anyone who didn't follow the club's ordinances. Needless to say, there was a time when Tom was quite the tough guy.

**Tom's Story-**

## It's All About The Bacon

I went to church every Sunday until my dad passed away when I was nine. After my dad died, my mom could care less if we went, so I fell away from the church. At the funeral, my mother blamed me for causing my father's death, and at that exact moment, somehow, I lost my ability to see colors. When I walked out of the funeral home, all I could see was black and white, like an old television movie. The burden of guilt placed upon me that day took the joy of color (and many other things) away from me. I was sad, color-blind, and bitter at the same time.

The older I got, the angrier I became, and as an adult, I joined a biker gang and did many things that I couldn't talk about. I finally left gang life and started managing a bar for a friend. While working at the bar, I met Kerri, with whom I have been married for 30 years by God's grace. We had our share of problems during our marriage, and in July 2008, we nearly divorced. I know there were at least three times when God supernaturally intervened directly in my life. Each time, He did something miraculous in order to get my attention.

The first time God stepped in, I was angry and knew my life with Kerri was ending. I really didn't want to live anymore. So, I got on my Harley and took off like a bat out of hell down the highway. As I approached a sharp bend in the road, I thought, "This is it." I took my hands off the handlebars and headed toward a large cluster of trees. With my throttle wide open and my hands at my side, the bike screamed right toward the trees. It was impossible not to hit one, as there were so many. I closed my eyes and waited to die, but God had other plans. I don't remember exactly what happened because I blacked out, but when I woke up, I was next to my bike on the side of the road. The bike's kickstand was down and just sitting there. I was shocked to see that there was no damage to the bike and not a single scratch on me. It wasn't humanly possible, but all things are possible with God.

A few days later, God got my attention again. I vividly remember sitting in my workshop on our farm in early July. It was a hot sunny day when a powerful force came over me out of nowhere. I was crying, shaking, and trembling, and I felt like I couldn't control myself. I literally thought I was going nuts. I called Connie, a friend of ours, and asked her to call my wife Kerri and ask her to come home. Connie called Kerri for me, but I didn't think she would bother leaving work since we were struggling and she had been keeping her distance, but thankfully she did come home. When Kerri got home, she asked me what was going on. I told her I loved her and was so sorry for everything I had done to her. But Kerri quickly replied, "I want a divorce." Right then, a calm came over me, and I knew if a divorce would make her happy, then so be it. I then went to a buddy's house to stay and try to get things sorted out, and that's when God showed up a third time.

While at my Buddy's place, things just didn't feel right. Something in my mind repeatedly said, "Tom, you need to go home," so I headed home immediately. When I got home, something was still wrong, and I knew it was our relationship. The next day, I didn't feel I could go to work because everything inside me felt fragile and shattered. I began to ask God for forgiveness, and I was shaken to the core of my being.

The battle became so intense that I eventually dropped down to my knees. I then felt a wave of peace come over my soul as I surrendered my anger and bitterness to God. My guilt and shame were taken away!

On that hot summer day, as I knelt and prayed, past lies were replaced by God's truth and peace. I opened my eyes and realized I could see the blue in the sky, the green grass, and the gorgeous trees. I knew God had healed me. He had created and sought me, and He wasn't letting go. Everything began to make sense. I looked around and wept, but these were happy tears streaming down my face. I was finally free from the demons that had controlled my life for so many years.

I then started praying and thanking God for a new life! I told my wife Kerri what had happened, and she praised God. She was truly happy and eventually decided to stay with me. Since all this has taken place, all kinds of things have happened to me. Kerri's prayers for me to find peace through God had happened, and my love for God and His truth has grown every day. Through this, my relationship with Kerri is now strong. But the most important thing that has occurred is that God gave me the gift of discerning spirits, as found in the book of 1 Corinthians 12. I have subsequently used these God-given abilities to help over a thousand people find freedom from their demonic oppression. It's been an incredible ride so far, and now I wake up each morning filled with joy and anticipation of how God will keep using me for His glory.

While Tom was giving his testimony, I can clearly recall looking past his left shoulder and vividly seeing angels in the room. These angels were shoulder to shoulder, beautifully white in color, each looking similar to the next and standing about twelve feet tall. They surrounded the room with all the men gathered in the circle. The peace that came over me during that experience is almost indescribable.

We lost Tom to a heart attack a few years ago. Tom was one of those guys that were rough around the edges but a teddy bear on the inside. I have often referred to Tom as a "Saul to Paul conversion on the road to Damascus" (Acts chapter 9). Tom wasn't seeking God, but God WAS seeking Tom. What an honor it was to know Tom and to be able to call him my friend.

## So What?

Finding the right study and watching how the Holy Spirit draws the men in is nothing short of life-transforming!

***"Ask, and it shall be given you; seek, and ye shall find; knock, and it shall be opened unto you."***
***~Matthew 7:7~***

## -16-
## Developing A Spiritual Leadership Team (S.A.L.T. Team)

When we first started the Men Under Construction group, life was simple. We would either go to a work night and "work" or a study night and "study." It was nothing too complicated. However, after a few years of doing life together with these guys, we began to realize that we should add more structure and meaning to all the aspects of what we were doing. Thus, we decided to create a Spiritual Leadership Team, or for those of you who like acronyms, S.A.L.T.

Our idea behind the SALT team was to assemble a small group of men I could bounce ideas off or canvas to see how the recent study night went. I ask things like, "How was the overall attitude of the guys during the work night." The team I was looking for were guys who could be harshly honest with me if that's what was needed. The last thing I wanted was a bunch of "Yes men" who would tell me what I wanted to hear.

I found that by having this group of critical-thinking men, I could hone every process of MUC that we offered. For example, if a study night dragged on or someone was grandstanding during a discussion, the group could point that out to me so I could improve it.

The same dynamics would apply to the work nights. If the projects weren't adequately prepped, or the scope of work wasn't clear enough, then the SALT guys would point this out to me and ultimately assist me in becoming a better leader.

    The initial men chosen for SALT were able to meet for a lunch break together on Tuesdays directly after the study/work night. We would say we were getting Tacos on Tuesday at noon and then meet at one of our favorite taco restaurants. So, not only did we meet and share thoughts and ideas, but we also enjoyed cheap tacos together. We did this for several years, and eventually, the "Taco Tuesday" event went from just the SALT team to all the MUC guys being invited. I still meet with my original SALT team, and they still provide the same level of input and critique. Still, the taco thing seems to be helping several of the MUC men who don't typically connect outside of the group to have an additional outlet for fellowship.

    Regarding the study night material deliberations, I will poll the SALT guys to see what they are discerning that the MUC group needs. Once I've heard their thoughts and ideas, I will look for a study guide incorporating their vision. Then once I have found a few books to consider, I take the idea and the prospective title of the study to the group as a whole and let them decide. It is amazing to see how well they participate and respond when they realize they are in control.

**So what?**

    Never ever go at it alone. Good leaders know to surround themself with people who are smarter or better than themselves. I couldn't lead well without these men, primarily because they also listen to what the Holy Spirit says. So often, I have received affirmation that the direction I sensed was the same as what the SALT team felt. That is a blessed moment when the "peace that passes all understanding" becomes extremely real.

**"And the peace of God, which surpasses all understanding, will guard your hearts and your minds in Christ Jesus."**
**~ Philippians 4:7~**

## -17-
# How To Celebrate And Acknowledge Each Other

At Men Under Construction, we've discovered how to spend time doing more together besides studying and working nights. We have typically done so much together that an occasional celebration of our accomplishments is warranted and even needed. Celebrating our yearly Anniversary, having an Annual Cookout, Christmas party, White Elephant Gift Exchange, and even an occasional birthday can be what it takes to keep the men engaged with each other. After all, even if they don't admit it, every man wants and needs to feel valued. Events like a steak cookout or an Anniversary Celebration are great opportunities for the church to show appreciation. It can also lend time for your guys to recognize each other.

In the church, the MUC group rarely gets any attention. Sure, many folks in our congregation have heard of MUC or Men Under Construction, but if asked, it's not very often that a person can name one of the MUC guys. One of the topics that frequently comes up in church is why the guys aren't publicly acknowledged for their work. We have often joked about how the MUC men are the elves that show up on Monday night and make the shoes. No one knows exactly who did the work or how complex the project was. All that is seen is the excellent result. We intentionally don't wish to draw attention to ourselves; instead, we affirm each other privately. This ongoing dynamic helps keep us humble and our work as a blessed offering. The stark reality is that anytime there's a church business-type meeting, most men who attend are the guys who would say they are affiliated with MUC but choose to keep our pride in check by staying as anonymous as possible.

**The Baconfest!**

Even the word "Baconfest" sounds delicious! I have learned that bacon is a universally accepted aphrodisiac for most men (including those vegetarian types of guys). Whenever we have a Baconfest, the objective is for everyone to bring a small to medium-sized dish to share that contains bacon within the ingredients.

I have seen bacon-wrapped jalapenos, bacon-wrapped Oreo cookies, baked beans with lots of bacon, little smokies wrapped in bacon, bacon dipped in dark chocolate, brownies covered in bacon bits, and cookies made with bacon grease. There are just so many delicious things that can be done with bacon! Prior to the actual Baconfest event, I'll cook up 2-3 pounds of strip thick cut bacon in the room where the event is being held, just to make sure that from the moment the guys enter the building, they will smell the bacon. They will know beyond a shadow of a doubt they are in the right place.

**Annual Steak Cookout**

We've been blessed to have an annual steak cookout every year, except for the first three years when we tried to invent ourselves. One of our original M.U.C. guys has a comfortable lake house out of town where we can meet for this event. In July or August, we will gather to cook and eat steaks along with some great side dishes. We also shoot guns, do some fishing, and grow in our relationships. I will tell you that through the years, we have been really blessed by our commitment to the church and each other. God continues to provide for the recognition that these guys mentally, emotionally, and physically need to keep trudging along week after week. In my opinion, there's not much better than hanging out with so many dedicated Muckleheads eating ribeye and telling stories. I've cherished each one of these nights and look forward to many more in the future.

**Christmas White Elephant Gift Exchange**

The silliest acknowledgment event I want to discuss is our Christmas White Elephant Gift Exchange. Each year we gather at the church's Family Life Center and start the night out with a Baconfest. Once we are all good and full of pork products, we will gather into a rather large circle in the middle of the room. If everyone has done their tasks correctly, there will be a pile of poorly wrapped gifts in the center of the circle that will perfectly match the number of men in attendance.

That's when the fun begins. If you're not familiar with a White Elephant Gift Exchange, the idea is for each guy to find something they own that has little to no value to them any longer, place that item in a box, wrap it in Christmas paper, and then watch and see who ends up with their former "treasure." The fun is accomplished by how a gift gets handed from guy to guy, sometimes even vengefully. Everyone gets a number that is drawn from a bucket. The person with the highest number is the luckiest because they get to choose their gift last. The first unlucky person grabs a gift from the pile in the center. They then unwrap it and must "proudly" display the trinket in front of them. The second person in line can either "steal" the first person's gift or get their own gift from the pile. Each time, the unwrapped gift needs to be displayed. This process goes on and on until the last guy gets a gift. The biggest catch here is that a gift can be stolen up to three times by the players. After the third time, the gift has found its final resting spot. I'll tell you, the creativity of the gifts and the orneriness of the guys can make it extremely hysterical. I've seen a jock strap setup to launch tennis balls, two-year-old calendars, rubber chickens, bacon-flavored gum, and toothpaste, all the way to antique hand tools. My all-time favorite is the screaming goat toy. There has never been a Christmas party with these guys when I haven't gone home with my sides aching from laughing so hard.

## Annual MUC Anniversary

The final acknowledgment event is our Annual MUC Anniversary. This night is by far the most emotional night of our gatherings. Yes, we start the night out with a Baconfest. But once the food is all done, then comes the real heartfelt moments. The guys will gather into a large circle, and that's when I get the opportunity to tell them all about their accomplishments for the year. I tell them how many hours they worked and how much money they saved the church. I highlight some of the past year's study topics and then talk about the MUC men who are no longer with us. You would think that I would have become hardened to these names by saying them year after year, but that's not the case.

I'll get to Danny, Tom, or Leonard, and my voice will crack. A tear will start to form in my eye, followed by long pauses as I attempt not to break down into a ball of emotions. I really get attached to all these guys, and once they're gone, nothing can replace them.

After all the statistics and memories have been accounted for, we move on to a special guest. Oftentimes, I'll ask one of the local pastors to come and speak. Our pastors know our MUC guys well, so they can easily relate to them through their personal storytelling. We then finish the night with communion together. And since we are Men Under Construction, we use manly pieces of bread and manly quantities of juice to celebrate communion together.

**So What?**

Being part of a large men's group can be so much more than just a weekly gathering. For many of us, it is really a daily thing. I will rarely go through the course of the day without two or three MUC guys contacting me. I find that this has never been a burden. We depend on each other. We have reached this point together because of our trust in each other. Acknowledging the men, making them feel special and cared for, and laughing and crying together are all fruitful attributes desperately needed to create strong friendships and unbreakable brotherly ties.

*"A new commandment I give to you, that you love one another: just as I have loved you, you also are to love one another. By this all people will know that you are my disciples."*
*~John 13:34-35 ESV~*

## -18-
# It's All About The Bacon

I know two things. In case you weren't aware of it, ALL MEN LOVE BACON! and "Sometimes you want to go where everybody knows your name, and they're always glad you came" (lyrics from the Cheers sitcom). With these two concepts, you can attract a plethora of men. It isn't so much about the bacon itself, but there is this ideology that bacon holds a special place in men's memories. Most of us grew up with that smell of bacon lofting from the kitchen early on a Sunday morning. Smelling this heavenly scent meant that someone cared enough to get the stove all greasy and have that odorous scent linger in the air for hours and hours. For me, the smell of bacon is true comfort. My wife and I love to camp, and camping without bacon is like Summer without flip-flops. The whole idea behind being successful with your group is that you need to know your men (We'll talk more about that later).

Marketing is essential to keeping any men's group together for any length of time. The moment that the focus is lost can also be that moment when momentum is lost as well.

If the marketing plan for your men's group is clear and easy to remember and reiterated by the rest of the men in the group, then recruiting should be a simple task. I've found that our best recruiters for MUC are the guys who love the vision and the companionship, and they understand we're all in this for a much bigger purpose. Another essential part of our plan is we have a simple logo that we place on all of our T-shirts and literature. The logo is an orange triangle (think construction work zone) with the Men Under Construction name and depicts a group of men performing construction-related items (There is an example of the logo at the end of the book). The men will receive a new T-shirt every year on our MUC Anniversary. We figure enough money has been saved through work nights that the costs of the T-shirts are covered many times over.

This past Summer, the church had a volunteer recruitment weekend where each department presented information regarding the available opportunities. We got a premium location for our booth right outside the front doors into the main lobby. To get the attention of men, we fried up several pounds of thick-cut maple-enhanced bacon and passed out packages of microwave popcorn with a small business-size card stapled to each packet. The card gave basic information, such as when to meet weekly, a simple vision statement, and contact information. Not even the shyest of men can resist free hot sizzling bacon!

**So What?**

It sounds cliche to refer to bacon and men constantly, but it is true. The smell of bacon is universally known in America. It simply represents comfort in a time when everything seems so chaotic. Bacon is the food that brings men together, whether it's sizzling at home, piled high on a hamburger, or part of a delicious treat during a Baconfest. Bacon brings us joy and can provide us with such a simple pleasure. I have found that all I have to say is "bacon," and every guy becomes my best friend!

*"I know that there is nothing better for people than to be happy and to do good while they live. That each of them*

It's All About The Bacon

*may eat and drink, and find satisfaction in all their toil—
this is the gift of God."
~Ecclesiastes 3:12-13~*

## -19-
# You're Always Welcome

Like the Prodigal son in the Bible (Luke 15), once you are part of the group, you're always part of the group. Regardless if you come and support it each week or haven't attended an event for over a year, once a MUC man, always a MUC man. If you really want to impact men, you can't keep score. We have some guys who only show up for the big events or just the study nights. Occasionally, some of the more regular guys might make remarks about the inconsistencies, but I generally reiterate this standard and deflect their concerns. Personally, I enjoy seeing each of these men whenever they show up. After all, who am I to judge? You never know when some issues and opportunities arise for some of these guys, and they can't consistently attend. Regardless, I feel it's my responsibility to also be there for them.

When we get together, we often joke that in order to be a man under construction, you need to have a dog, a beard, and/or a gun. It really comes down to a willingness to be open to friendships, accountability, faith in God, and a strong passion for the taste of bacon (sarcasm). Our group currently consists of men from our church, along with others from five or so other churches. I don't see any issues with this as long as a passion for connecting with each other and God is the common denominator. And who knows, having a couple of men from other congregations could potentially create replication in their churches as well. Isn't that what Men Under Construction is all about? Disciples are making other disciples.

As with most groups, you'll always have guys who come and go and then come back again. I have two stories regarding two guys who fit into this category. Both men are wonderful people, and we are so blessed to have them in our group AND to be there for them when they need support.

**Jim's Story–**

**A Lost Soul Who Found a Home**

Jim first showed up at one of our MUC study nights in 2006. To say Jim was rough around the edges was an understatement. Even so, Jim always had a smile. However, Jim knew how to throw down some sarcasm. Jim constantly struggled with self-esteem and would often move from job to job, each time looking for acceptance and some sort of stability. We often heard about how the "Manager didn't like him" or that some other employee was out to make him look bad. Jim used the social systems to survive and drift through life. Jim was married but lived in a separate location due to his financial situation. The issue with Jim was that he had a lot of demons on his back, so much so that he would constantly be struggling with his communication skills. These demons did everything they could to mess with Jim's concentration and focus.

One day, about two years after he started hanging out with the guys, Jim went to a spiritual deliverance ministry session (Wellsprings of Freedom Ministries), and wow, what a difference! I vividly remember holding a conversation with Jim the day after his first session. We talked for an hour about life, his job, and his wife. Jim was so easygoing and very knowledgeable about lots of guy-type stuff, yet I wouldn't call him the slightest bit mechanical. Nonetheless,

Jim was a great part of the MUC group. One Easter, we were building a prop for the Good Friday production. We came up with the idea of creating a 20-foot tall by a 16-foot-wide wooden cross. We decided to build this cross so that it appeared to be three feet thick from top to bottom. So, we got creative, and since I hate the idea of building something once and then destroying it so shortly afterward, we chose to build a bunch of boxes stacked on each other. These boxes would eventually become road cases for future storage. These boxes were 4-foot wide by 3-foot deep by 3-foot high and each with a lid. We then stacked and screwed these cases together to create that rather large cross. We convinced Jim that the cross was so top-heavy that we needed some substantial weight for the base until we could get the cross appropriately supported from the trusses.

We talked Jim into climbing into the bottom road case, and then we screwed the door shut. It seemed like a funny prank at first until we unscrewed the door, and Jim didn't want to come out.

He said it was one of the most peaceful places he had ever been. Jim kind of deflated our sails, but on the other hand, this experience opened up my eyes to the depth of Jim's patience and his search for the peace that only the Holy Spirit (and a small, confined space) could provide.

Jim died from a head injury in 2011, which left a big hole in the MUC group. Even though he was a bit odd and seemed a little out of place, he still was one of the MUC guys and will be sorely missed. On our 18th MUC Anniversary, Jim's sister sent us a letter regarding the impact that MUC had on Jim's life. I tried reading the letter to the guys during that year's Anniversary celebration, but I couldn't. Thankfully one of the guys grabbed the letter and got the job done. Here's what Jim's sister had to say.

## It's All About The Bacon

There's a song called "Thank You" that was made popular by Ray Boltz. It tells the story of someone experiencing their first day in Heaven and meeting people who are blessed somehow by their life. One of the verses goes like this.

> *"One by one they came*
> *far as the eye could see*
> *Each life somehow changed*
> *By your generosity*
> *Little things that you had done*
> *Sacrifices made*
> *Unnoticed on the Earth*
> *In Heaven now proclaimed"*

I can tell you the names of two people who will come running to meet you, and I'm one of them. Whenever I think of the MUC group, I literally get tears in my eyes because I witnessed how you helped my brother Jim. What you did for Jim, you did for me. We've all read the story of the Good Samaritan. You were the Good Samaritan to my brother.

You found him in the dirt, beaten up by the world, and you offered him a place at the table. You gave him what no man had ever given him before. You gave him friendship, acceptance, and brotherly love.

My brother Jim went home to be with the Lord eleven years ago this month. I sometimes dream about my first day in Heaven. Once I manage to turn my eyes from my Lord, I will run to my brother's arms. I have the assurance in my heart that Jim is there because he responded to God's love on this earth. Our Lord used MUC to demonstrate that loving

God and loving each other is what it's all about. So, on this your Anniversary, I say to you.

*Thank you for giving to the Lord*
*Jim and I are lives that were changed*
*Thank you for giving to the Lord*
*We are so glad you gave!*

**Greg's Story-**

In 2007, after twelve years of marriage, my wife decided to get a divorce. I was beside myself, insecure about who I was, my role as a single father of two, and how I would manage a household on my own. I had quit a job prior to the divorce as she claimed that my working a second shift position was an issue. So, I went to work at another company only to discover I was highly allergic to some of the products they produced. So now I was without a job and quickly slipping into depression. I couldn't eat or sleep. I could barely get myself out of the house. Thankfully I was able to get rehired by my previous employer except for half of the pay. This drop in income only added to my deepening spiral into the darkness of depression. That is when I forced myself to return with a group of men I had initially met around 2004. The name of the group was Men Under Construction. I managed to make it to church one weekend while all of this was happening. While at church, a dear friend told me that I needed to stay in church and not give up. I took this to mean "stay involved with the MUC group."

On one of the nights that the guys were holding a Bible study, I found myself deeply intent on listening to the hurts of some of the other men. I found that I could really relate to their situation.

There were many times I wanted to give up and not be here anymore, but I just kept going and did my best to take one day at a time. One of the guys told me, "Yes, today looks hopeless. Try to make it through one day, then two days, then a week, a month, and soon a year will have passed. You'll look back at that time and think "yeah, that sucked" but you'll be in a whole different and hopefully better place." I had seen other guys who were also in my shoes through the MUC group, and I could see how much better their life had gotten. They weren't perfect or had that "perfect sort of life," but they were progressing in who they were becoming. I learned that progression only comes when people are authentic in who they are and willing to share their struggles. Men must share what they are wrestling with and be called out in love for their B.S. I am genuinely thankful for my MUC brothers in Christ who spoke into my and my children's lives.

Life is so much better now. I am remarried and in such a good place. I am in a place where I can help others now. And speaking of helping others, I hold a fond memory of what happened a few years after my divorce. The MUC guys were doing a big demolition project at one of our campuses. I brought my son with me that night. It was an awesome opportunity to work side-by-side with him. We still talk about that special time of our lives.

## So what?

We have all learned that everyone is important. No one is more important than the other. We found that the impact can be so far-reaching by accepting everyone for who they are and allowing the Holy Spirit to work in their life. In this case, Jim's life change reached all through his family and who knows how much further.

***"Finally, all of you, be like-minded, be sympathetic, love one another, be compassionate and humble."***
***~1 Peter 3:8~***

## -20-
# What's Said At M.U.C. Stays At M.U.C.

One of our mantras is, "What's said at MUC stays at MUC." Of course, we based this on the preverbal "What happens in Vegas stays in Vegas," but that's not our intent. Our goal is to create a space where transparency is the norm. This is where everyone gets the chance to speak, where everyone's voice is just as important as the next guy's. I've learned (rather quickly) that if I am transparent and willing to point out my flaws, I've frequently observed that others will follow suit. Some of the most impactful study nights we have ever experienced are when individuals open up and share their hurts freely, even knowing they could be ridiculed by the world's standards. When we say, "What happens at MUC stays at MUC," we mean that our nights together are free from judgment. No one is ever going to use what you've said against you. This night and these men are as safe as it will get. To this day, this simple phrase hasn't been broken. Below is a story and testimony of Tom. Tom found that transparency provides a level of freedom that leaves Satan powerless against the sins of his past. Tom's willingness to share his story has shown several other men that it's OK, to be honest, and that the truth doesn't make you any less of a man.

**Tom's Story-**
**What Honesty and Transparency Looks Like**

I was born the fifth of six kids in 1966. True grace and forgiveness have allowed me to overcome the obstacles put in front of me in my childhood. My father left his disaster of a home at 16 with his mother's consent to join the Army. Driven in life, he achieved the position of instructor at the West Point Academy. Needless to say, I grew up in a military household. He would leave lists of things to do for us daily, fifty push-ups, sit-ups, pull-ups, and run. We had best do whatever he instructed us to do. He always worked two jobs and was never around.

From my earliest memories, I recall my mother's hateful comments to us, like, "Having kids ruined her life, we were cursed in life, and we were her punishment from God, and on and on." There was never any I love you, hugs or feeling of value. We received nothing but the complete opposite. I recall one occasion when my dad had me pinned against a wall in the kitchen.

My mom screamed, "Stop!" My hope quickly disappeared when she said, "Give me his glasses. I'm not going to pay to get him new ones if they break." So, he handed her my glasses, and she walked away, and he continued.

By the time I was ten, I worked delivering newspapers at a vegetable farm and other odd things to pay my way through life. I paid for my Little League registration, gloves, clothes, etc.

Imagine my surprise when my dad found over 16 thousand dollars in a cigar box. That's when I realized that my mom had stashed the money away throughout the years. All those years of "being a burden and a drain on my parents" and being broke were nothing more than a lie.

As I entered adulthood, I questioned how long I would live. I was not nurtured or taught to have any internal value. Education for me was hindered by severe ADHD. I had a wild and defiant streak and the drive inherited from my dad. We went to church in my childhood as my dad ironically became a deacon. My mom played the organ at church as well, and we put this false front in public of normalcy, which made me feel dirty. This hypocrisy also made me feel guilty because God knows all, so He certainly cannot love me.

As a young adult, I met a "damsel in distress." We ended up getting married (not my best or clearest choice, but hell, as worthless as I was, I was lucky to find anyone). We welcomed twin girls into the world at 26 weeks. Due to an emergency cesarean section, I sadly had to watch one of my daughters die as the other struggled. The struggle of losing our daughter and our poor choices eventually led the marriage to fail. I came home from work to find my house completely empty with no prior idea of trouble. My now ex-wife made it almost impossible for me to see my daughter. I felt I was useless, and this was what I deserved.

I then met Kim. She was beautiful, kind, and funny and was as broken on the inside as I was. We were married, and life was good. We now have two kids, and because of the struggles and deficiencies I previously had, I am a more loving, caring, and supportive dad. My kids are going to have a good life to look back on. God gave me a chance to rewrite what I knew with these two gifts from Him.

By this time, I had built a physical persona of 250 lbs. and was not quite ugly, to boot. Unfortunately, I had gained a prideful false image of power about myself. Then my son was severely injured during a wrestling tournament. There were no answers, and I remember within the first week of his injury, he felt that he could not go on anymore because there was no answer or solutions for his future. Prayer chains, begging God to take me and heal him, pleading to

God for help left me wondering, "Is this just another thing I deserve?"

My daughter also suffered as she did not want to burden Kim or me with her issues and made some very bad decisions. I feel that I let her down and failed her. My boy's medical condition is like a horror movie. It's like you do not know where or when, but the fear of potential death could be around any corner at any moment.

I went to the church we were attending during a bad time of my son's injury. I sat there and wept while the building was empty during the week, only to be confronted in a not-very-kind way about what I was doing there. I realized that my whole life was affected by flawed people but not by a flawed God. I finally accepted and embraced God, not my parents, who put me here. My purpose now and the gift of empathy is to seek out others in pain and use my pain experience to give them the strength to go on.

I have learned that suffering creates humility, which in turn, with love, creates awareness for others. Suffering and being a victim are not the same. Everyone suffers if they have a pulse. It is the price of admission for life. The battle to conquer and not give in to being a victim makes one able to continue to love, care, and have hope even in the pitch of darkness.

I have evolved to now having total trust in God's plan. He put me here and will take me out when He wants me. If I were to die tomorrow knowingly, I would thank Him for what He gave me and look forward to what lies ahead. Jesus was sent to earth and suffered tremendously, and I believe He did this to show us His example of how to live and embrace one's suffering as He did, never letting it make you love God or others less in the process.

## So What?

When your group develops trust with each other, that's when the stories of life can be told without judgment or any sort of adverse reaction. Tom was incredibly transparent, freely opening his heart and exposing his scars to our group. We all cherish Tom; honestly, we now have a better understanding of some of his quirks. The other miracle of Tom's story was that he wasn't alone. At least one of the guys told him that his life mirrored Tom's. This openness and sharing have allowed several other guys the willingness to bear their hearts and scars.

*"Yet the Lord longs to be gracious to you; therefore he will rise up to show you compassion. For the Lord is a God of justice. Blessed are all who wait for him!"*
*~Isaiah 30:18~*

## On a lighter side - "What's Said at MUC Stays at MUC" Applies to Work Nights Too!

One night a few years back, in the middle of prop-making for an upcoming Easter service, I overheard a conversation between a couple of the guys: "Bob, what's your wife going to say when you tell her you did Paper Mache at MUC tonight?" Bob confidently replied, "I'm not telling her. What happens at MUC stays at MUC!"

## -21-
# The Role Of The Leader

What does it take to be the one that's helping the group along?

- You must be willing to make and own mistakes when they happen.
- Be capable of Identifying the work projects and have some sort of game plan.
- Be able to pull the group together when it comes to problem-solving.
- A basic understanding of typical construction methods helps, or having those around you who know how to get things done. I find that I don't need to know everything. I just need someone who knows and can share that knowledge.
- Identify the "next" study or be able to present multiple study topics to the group in order to gain consensus.
- Be transparent - Transparency creates trust. Your guys need to know they can trust you. We will talk about this more later in the book.
- Always place the other guys' needs in front of your own.
- Manage time correctly - It's always a struggle to keep everything flowing like it should while keeping an eye on the clock. Constantly running overtime can create unnecessary tension.
- Always be thankful - be eager to look for the good in all situations.

- Be a planner - be thinking a month or two out. What's our next study topic? What's our next work night look like? When was the last time we had a fun night or celebrated our accomplishments?
- Be an encourager - Good job! I really appreciate you!
- Communication is essential. Depending on your group's demographics, send weekly emails and Facebook posts about what's coming up.
- Have some way of interacting with the church management so you know the desired goals and wishes of those who make the top decisions.
- Empower others to recruit and be responsible for continuously growing the group. Our best recruiters are the MUC guys who wholeheartedly believe in the group's mission.
- Know the guys - which we'll talk about in the next chapter.

**So what?**

Read on to the next chapter.

## -22-
# Know And Grow The Men In Your Group

How many of your guys are Veterans? How many are divorced? Who has been married the longest? Are any of the men widowers? How many of the men have experienced great loss, such as suicide or cancer?

When you are first starting your church group, knowing your men's life experiences can take quite a bit of time. I wish I could provide you with a surefire way of gaining this knowledge more expeditiously, but I can't. Ultimately, the guys need to freely open up and trust you with the deepest knowledge about themselves. However, there are a few things that I have learned along the way. First, if you tell them about yourself, they will feel more comfortable telling you about themself. Be transparent and show your flaws; eventually, they'll do the same. Look for similarities in your group and capitalize on those connections. Ask direct questions, like how long have you been married? Do you have children? Did you serve in the military? The more you ask, the more you'll know. Trust that the Holy Spirit will guide you and provide the knowledge that can only come from above. Constantly work on gaining their trust. This process isn't a once-and-done dynamic. Also, remember the old saying, "Honesty is the best policy," which still holds true. Especially in today's world, when it seems like lying or twisting the truth is okay, and it is no longer chastised, honesty feels like a gust of fresh air.

There was a time when I knew what sort of soda pop every guy liked. It may seem like such a small thing, but when you're dripping with sweat, and the leader passes you your favorite beverage, enough said. Once you get to know the men, you can also pick out who the natural leaders are. Figuring out who can lead makes life so much easier, especially when pairing guys up for work nights or when you're taking a vacation. Finding someone to fill in as the leader is the difference between canceling a week or keeping things rolling.

Not long ago, I passed off the reins to another guy for a study night. The guy's name is Kevin (Big Kevin). For the most part, everyone knew how the night should go. The guys set up the chairs, kept the night on schedule, harassed each other, shared openly, enjoyed dessert and fellowship, and really didn't miss a beat. Big Kevin has that level of passion and care that makes the rest of the men feel comfortable. His leadership skills allowed me to take some vacation time and know I was leaving the group in highly capable hands. Every leader should look for that next leader they can nurture and develop, then finally release to replicate whatever the goal is.

Here's a story about another guy I saw so much potential in. His name is Tim.

**Tim's Story–**
**Identify, Empower, and Release**

Tim started with the MUC group in early 2005. He was a High School teacher with a healthy passion for the kids that many would give up on. Those that would sadly fall through the cracks if nobody intervened. He worked in some of the most challenging schools in our area. Because of his drive to make a difference in the underprivileged kids, Tim learned patience, perseverance, and how to invest in someone regardless of how rough their conditions were.

Tim had heard about the Men Under Construction group from a few other guys he knew that attended. He was looking for a group to help him balance the chaos in his life. The first night Tim came to MUC, he was dressed in his school/work clothes, and of course, that night was a work night. Tim decided to join in anyway as we tore out walls and ceilings at our main campus in preparation for a remodel of our lobby area.

Tim recalled how foreign it was to him to see all of these men laughing and joking while at the same time swinging sledgehammers. Tim was raised in a family were using your hands and tools just didn't happen. Regardless, he jumped right in, and in more ways than just construction!

About two years into the group, Tim was asked to close a study night in prayer. Despite having little experience with eloquent prayer, Tim prayed just like he was talking face-to-face with our Creator. The next step for Tim was to lead the group while my wife and I were on vacation. I could see in him that he had the desire and the passion for leading, and the Holy Spirit had gifted him with the ability to nurture the men. One night afterward, Tim and I had a great heart-to-heart talk about his feelings. He and I felt it was time for him to step away from MUC and start another men's group. Tim was surprised when he told me about his new calling, that the whole time I was shaking my head up and down. We both knew in our hearts that he needed to go and spread his wings.

Since that day in 2008, Tim has started a Tuesday morning class, led a local men's outreach group, went to other churches and started men's groups, and so much more.

Tim is truly an awesome example of discipling, identifying, empowering, and releasing, but still maintaining excellent communication so that he can freely pour back into his roots when needed or desired.

## So What?

Being the Christ-centered leader of men is a daunting task but so worth it. Especially when you feel you get more out of it than the guys do. Every leader should be actively looking for a replacement. Things come up, vacations and emergencies happen, and burnout is always a concern. The sooner leaders identify others they can raise up to lead and co-lead, the better and stronger the group dynamics will be, and God's work will blossom.

The other night someone said, "Where else can 40 guys get together, talk honestly, and openly share their feelings, all while genuinely trusting each other, and no alcohol was involved?"

> *"Just as I have loved you, you also are to love one another. By this all people will know that you are my disciples, if you have love for one another."*
> *~John 13:34-35~*

## -23-
# The Short Version

Since most guys I know don't like to read a lot; I've included a summary of this book - something that's more to the point with fewer words.

**1. What is the Idea Behind Men Under Construction?**

Every thriving church needs a strong group of volunteers to assist in maintaining and repairing the church's properties. The thought behind a group such as Men Under Construction or M.U.C. was to have a group that would alternate weekly gatherings between a Work Night and a Study Night. This alternating meeting time eliminates burnout and creates a stronger emphasis on community and fellowship. Another benefit to having an alternating weekly event would be that there is a two-week amount of time to assess the maintenance needs of the facilities. These two weeks also allow for better planning and more thoughtful preparation for complex tasks. Regarding the Study Nights, the two-week period allows for quality study time and better preparation for teaching the subject matter.

When there isn't sufficient work to be done or a study subject hasn't yet been identified, we take breaks by enjoying a night of fellowship. These nights are typically called "Baconfest." A Baconfest is where each guy is asked to bring a bacon-themed dish to share. A Baconfest is a great time to cast some vision about upcoming projects, discuss possible study subjects, and discover what the men want to learn about. Ultimately the intent of any non-study/work night should be to provide an opportunity that's meaningful and respects each man's time that they are willing to commit to the church.

## 2. How Do You Get a Men's Group Started?

When we first started, we used the church's bulletin to advertise that a new men's group was forming. Whatever medium the church uses to communicate upcoming events to its congregation can be used. One of the simpler advertising methods we've used was to create a two-sided business card with the logo, a general description of the group, the meeting times, and contact information for the leader. These cards seem to work well since any man can keep a few of them in their wallet and easily pass them out when the opportunity presents itself.

The most crucial part of getting started is ensuring your group name and plan are clear and straightforward. Regarding the name and logo for Men Under Construction, *please feel free to use them.*

This group was created to attract men and draw them into a level of commitment to their church and each other. We've seen where the logo and name resonate well with the majority of men.

The only drawback to the name I have run across is when a guy feels they need to be handy or have some construction skills to be part of the group. Yes, it does take a bit of reasoning to dispel this idea. The usual response is that "Every man is under construction." It's not that one needs to be able to do construction.

We have also used email and social media platforms like Facebook to get the word out. We've created a FB page that is updated weekly with the upcoming events, such as Work Night or Study Night, and the plan for that night. Of course, a Baconfest night would have a video of sizzling hot bacon as an enticing feature. We have opened the Facebook "Men Under Construction" page to both men and women. Many times, the spouses of our men will catch information about the upcoming night quicker than the guys will and remind them of it. We also have a sizable email list of the guys (both active and inactive). Every Thursday or Friday morning, a simple email will go out with a message something like this:

**Header:** This upcoming Monday night is a work night

Guys, this upcoming Monday night is a work night.
Here's a list of the projects we have available to work on.

- Building a prop for the children's department
- Spreading mulch in the flower beds
- Assembling new bookshelves

- Reorganizing the tool room

We're looking for someone to help with the dessert as well.

Please let me know if that's you.

Blessings

One of the most impactful advertising things we've done was to create a simple T-shirt with the M.U.C.'s name on the front. Being at a church event where half the guys wear their MUC T-shirts is awesome.

## 3. Work Night Versus Study Night

Work nights are just that. It's a night where we gather together and do maintenance projects or prop and stage design for areas around our properties. Study nights are nights when we spend time in God's Word. On the study nights, we focus on men-type subjects. We have read through books like Revelation and James or studied how to have stronger relationships as men. We also have a time of accountability and connection at the tail end of the meetings.

## 4. Setting Up for a Work Night

Work nights take a good amount of preparation. It is essential to have the materials on hand before the work night begins. A visual design or picture of the finished product is invaluable. I will occasionally add a property map and indicate the projects' locations. Whatever the project is, it needs to be planned out properly. The materials for the projects need to be laid out appropriately, the men need to have a clear understanding of what is expected, and it helps if all the tools for the project are also readily available, including extension cords, ladders, hand tools, and garbage cans.

## 5. How a Work Night Should Function

I have found that starting with a collective gathering followed by a verbal accounting of the tasks for the evening is by far the best way to make the guys comfortable. It also allows the men to wrap their heads around what they are about to do. The next step is to team up the men with an appropriate partner or to divide the men into groups. It all depends on the size of the projects, or the skill set of the men in relation to the difficulty of the project. The men should then grab the supplies and tools for their designated project and head out to work. My task (or your task) is to move between the groups, ensuring they all have what they need, provide coaching, additional supplies, and water bottles, and provide any guidance that may be required.

## 6. Work Night Wrap-up

Everything seems to be moving smoothly, and a few guys are back at the starting point because they have finished their tasks. This is when the leader should make one last trip around to determine how complete the projects are. If everything went well and the planning was done properly, then the decisions should be easily made regarding what happens next for the uncompleted tasks. Can the project wait for two more weeks until the next work night, or is it better to gather the guys together to put everything you have into wrapping up that uncompleted project that evening?

### 7. Dessert and Fellowship

The work night is done, all the men have gathered back at the starting point, and the stories of what went well or not so well are flowing freely. Now is the time for the leader to go to work serving his men. We figured out about a year into MUC that every event needed to be wrapped up with a dessert. The desserts have ranged from cookies and cupcakes to delicious homemade pies and cakes.

I've observed that our guys aren't really picky. They're just hungry. I'll have a case or two of bottled water, a pot of hot coffee, and a cake provided by a volunteer sliced up and plated.

Often the guys will stick around another hour or so, spending time fellowshipping and enjoying each other's company. This dessert and fellowship time is the leader's time to let his guys know how much they are appreciated. I love serving the guys, and I believe they also enjoy it.

### 8. Setting up for a Study Night

It's a study night, and the guys will arrive in half an hour. Where do you start? First, grab enough chairs to seat the guys (I love guessing how many will show and how close I can get to being exact). One of the things that I learned from the pastor who initially hired me was that it is better to have to add chairs rather than have too many chairs. He said that there was always a bit of excitement that was created by having to add additional chairs as the event progressed, and I genuinely believe that he was correct.

The last setup requirement is to set up tables and chairs for the food and fellowship time after the study time is finished. Now ensure you have your study material, name tags, whiteboard and markers, and computer ready to go. If you get all that done in thirty minutes, you are a rock star!

## 9. Picking the Study Topic

I want to start this subject by recognizing that if you are not wholly dependent on the Holy Spirit for guidance, then don't expect much success. You need to know who your audience is, who your men are, where they are in life, and what kind of struggles they may be going through. Ask for guidance from the Holy Spirit in this regard and ask the men direct Spirit-lead questions.

If this is your first study and you don't know who your men are, I would suggest starting with the book of James. In James's first chapter, you'll come across the verse that states, "If you need wisdom, ask our generous God, and he will give it to you" (James 1:5). This is a great place to start since we all need wisdom. Ask for wisdom, and God will deliver wisdom, and you will be well on your way!

Regarding study guides, stick with simple guides with more questions than words. We have done a few studies that required too much reading (more than two pages worth), and a few things generally happen. The guys begin to glaze over, or the focus of the study gets lost in words. I have used a bunch of Steven Arterburn's studies. His guides are simple to follow, and each chapter in the guide is divided into two parts. Each part has six to ten questions that are really well thought out.

We have studied over 60 books since we started in 2004. We have covered every book in the New Testament at least once (Revelation, Romans, and James have been poured over twice). We have also studied Spiritual Warfare a few times, as well as Understanding World Religions, How to Forgive Yourself, and How to Tell Your Story (how to craft your testimony).

## 10. How a Study Night Should Function

The room begins to fill up with a variety of men of various ages. Initially, everyone sits at the front tables until the leader asks them to move to the study area. (When seated at tables, there is too much of a possibility for a few guys to become disconnected). All the chairs in the study area are in one large circle, so everyone faces each other. Being able to look every man in the eye is invaluable. The leader can sit within the group, stand and walk around it as they help the guys navigate the study, or sit in an elevated chair to be easily viewed (all are acceptable).

We always have a non-study night subject prior to starting prayer to do some quick "housekeeping." During this brief section, we will also talk about next week's work night or something newsworthy that would get lost if brought up at the end of the evening. Next, we'll open the night with prayer, asking the Holy Spirit to open our eyes and ears to what is being said. Then we jump right into the study.

## 11. Study Night Wrap-up

The first part of the study night is done. You've poured over the subject material and had fantastic heart-rendering discussions, so what's next? Once we've finished our study, I'll end by thanking the guys for listening so well and adding their input into the evening. Then we roll into the "How are you doing" section of our evening. I will then pick out a random guy around the circle and move clockwise. This section of time is when each man in the group gets an opportunity to ask for prayer, state a praise, or to ask for prayer for someone else. If everything is going great for the guy in the "hot seat," then a simple "I'm doing fine" works wonderfully, and we move on to the next man.

This activity is frequently another one of those moments when the Holy Spirit shows Himself and His touch on the group oh so well. By the time we get to the last guy in the circle, we frequently identify someone who needs extra care and attention. I love these moments because they present an opportunity to come together as a brotherhood of tightly bonded men to pray over a hurting brother. We often set a chair in the middle of the circle, gather around our brother, and lift his needs up in prayer, effectively placing them at the foot of the Cross. This exercise has substantially led to some amazing testimonials.

## 12. Dessert and Fellowship

WOW! What a great night of ministry! You've listened to the Word of God, discovered what the Holy Spirit wants you to hear, and listened to the hearts and prayers of your men. What's left? DESSERT, of course!

Once we wrap up in prayer, we'll break from the circle and head to the front tables and chairs. The leader now has the chance to serve the men a dessert that a volunteer (hopefully a spouse of one of the men) has lovingly prepared for the evening. Our MUC group has several men who like to bake, so coming up with an excellent dessert takes nothing more than an email request for help. During the dessert time, I witnessed deep one-on-one conversations and connections being made that typically wouldn't happen if the heart of the men hadn't been softened by the events of the evening.

The last thing that happens is that the men put the chairs and tables away, as well as a quick clean up. Since we are the servants of the church, the last thing you want is a reputation for leaving a mess.

## The Final So What?

It doesn't matter whether it is a work or study night. Each event requires great attention to set up and implement. Being the leader could be a reasonably intense position but with incredible benefits. Not only can you improve the quality of the maintenance at your church, but you can also use your men's skills to create intensive stage designs and props, thus making your church more attractive to your congregation and community. Additionally, when it comes to spiritual growth, the study nights will become a sacred time of connection, openness, and transparency that, sadly, many men will never experience in their lifetime.

Personally, I have found that I need the MUC men and our relationships to keep me on the straight and narrow path. I depend on these men in every aspect of my daily life. Never does a day go by that I haven't connected with at least

Kevin Herrick

one of them. I can honestly say I get as much out of Men Under Construction as any other man in the group.
    Thank You, Lord, and Amen!

It's All About The Bacon

# **NOTES**

Kevin Herrick

**NOTES**

It's All About The Bacon

# **NOTES**

Made in the USA
Columbia, SC
22 June 2023